Prophecy:

God's Divine Communications Media

By

Dr. Paula A. Price

Flaming Vision Publications
Tulsa, Oklahoma

Unless otherwise indicated, all scriptural quotations are from the *King James Version* of the Bible.

Prophecy: God's Divine Communications Media
Flaming Vision Publications
Tulsa, Oklahoma
ISBN 1-886288-03-8

Table of Contents

CHAPTER ONE

Cultivating a Prophetic Mindset

It is next to impossible to learn or value the prophetic unless one confronts his or her mindset on the subject. Years of evangelism, the ministry of the teacher, and charismata has virtually driven the prophetic underground. While God is persistently forcing its reinstitution upon us over the next several decades, the church has responded with tradition and a myriad of reactions ranging from ignoring what the Lord is apparently declaring is the next wave of His church to accepting in measured degrees crude regulation of the ministry.

How & Why Pastors Regulate the Prophetic

Pastors for any number of reasons have taken to rigidly regulating how the prophet functions in their churches. Much of their doctrine has been reactionary, aiming to protect the flock from uneducated, errant, or reckless prophets. Recognizing the need for the minister on some level by the way their congregations respond to the prophetic, the result has been to discredit the prophet's voice, intentionally or not.

Rules and regulations largely define the ministry and historical horrors identify the mantle.

People who have been adversely affected by the prophet's ministry have lodged all sorts of complaints against the ministry with their pastors. In response, the pastors, eager to remedy the problem, ignore the centuries of good the mantle has done over its years—even millennia—of service to God. All this is to say that what is considered modern prophetic genre mostly grew out of conflict, fear, and retaliation. None of these makes for a positive or reliable assessment of the officer and its mantle.

Where We Are Today Prophetically

The last decade or so of the twentieth century closed with studious prophetic exploration and the explosion of teachings to help the evangelical minded church learn the prophetic and better receive its ministry in action. These efforts are to be applauded, even though many of them overlooked the root of the problem. That is, the mindset of many of those correcting the problem is evangelical and those to whom they are writing are also steeped in the evangelist's mentality. While this statement is not meant to undermine the great work the evangelist's office has done over the years, it does point our corrective efforts in a sounder direction. Remedies must begin where their obstacles formed. With the prophetic, that is with the doctrine and theology of the declining move.

It is virtually impossible to prepare people for the prophetic apart from helping them locate the source of their resistance to it. Doing so requires awakening today's Christian soul to the layers of prophetic contempt that may be dormant in their subconscious. They must be made aware of some of the strategies previous church leaders unwittingly used against the prophets of their day that still work against them in the traditional mind of today's church. To grasp the scope of the problem consider the following facts and statistics concerning the prophet.

New Testament Prophetic Stats & Facts

1. The prophetic has been discredited since the medieval years of the Christian church, who responded to real or imagined abuses by waging war against it.
2. Much doctrine has been disseminated to so call, "warn people" against the prophetic. The warnings themselves have terrified many Christians into shutting down the prophetic in their world.
3. Most commentaries and expositories on the prophetic are **not** written by prophets.
4. Those regulating the office's activities have no idea about what it is to hear or respond to God as a prophet.
5. The New Testament identifies no pastoral contributions to the Bible's writings. Peter says the scriptures are emphatically prophetic. This truth mildly invalidates pastoral intervention in the crises and their subsequent regulation of prophetic ministry.
6. The majority of the scriptures were written by prophets with the exception of the New Testament, written by apostles.
7. Jesus came as a prophet, the Great Prophet to come foretold by Moses. See John 6:14; Acts 3:23; Deuteronomy 18:15, 18.
8. The prophet's is the oldest office of the five-fold ministers listed in Ephesians 4:11, according to Luke 11:50, 51.
9. God's revelatory mysteries are declared by His prophets. See Ephesians 3:5; Revelation 10:7; 22:6.
10. Revelation 22:9 says that there are prophetic angels.

11. The prophet(s) and the prophetic are translated in the Bible well over 4,000 times, including references to prophecy, prophesying, the word of the Lord and the numerous "thus saith." Our final research count topped 7,000 references.
12. Luke 24:35 canonizes the prophet's writings with Moses, a prophet, along with the Law and the Psalms, which were largely attributed to David, also a prophet. See also Matthew 26:56; Acts 2:29, 30; and Romans 16:26.
13. At least eight specific Old Testament prophets are mentioned and regarded in the New Testament by the Lord Jesus and once by Paul. Old Testament prophets named in the New Testament are listed below:
    1. Isaiah
    2. Jeremiah
    3. Jonah
    4. Daniel
    5. Joel
    6. Samuel
    7. Elijah
    8. David
14. Acts 11:27, 28 says that the Jerusalem church was staffed with prophets that came to Antioch.
15. Acts 15:32 states that the Antioch church was also staffed with prophets.
16. The New Testament names nine prophets, including the following:
    - Barnabas
    - Simeon
    - Niger
    - Lucius
    - Manaen

- Silas
- Agabus
- Judas
- John the Baptist

These exclude the two prophets in Revelation.

17. The Bible distinguishes prophets of the Lord as holy. See 2 Peter 3:2 and Revelation 22:6.
18. Luke 13:28 presents Abraham, Isaac, and Jacob as prophets that are joined by all the others in the kingdom of God. That kingdom would be that of the Lord Jesus Christ since God's only other kingdom on earth is that of the nation of Israel.
19. John the Baptist is the first New Testament prophet. He was prophesied to come by Malachi, the prophet, in Malachi 4:5.
20. Modern doctrine is to agree with the writings of the prophets; Acts 15:15.
21. Prophets are agents of God's government and order as seen in the number of times they are linked to the law:
    - Matthew 7:12
    - Matthew 22:40
    - Luke 16:16
    - John 1:45
    - Acts 13:15
    - Acts 24:14
    - Romans 3:21
22. Seven times the New Testament links the Law of Moses with the word and work of God's prophets. Here are five of them extracted from the seven references in the New Testament:
    - The golden rule, as it is called, is based on the law and the prophets.

- The two greatest love commandments of scripture, love for God and love for the fellowman, stem from the Law and the Prophets.
- Jesus' coming was according to the Law of Moses and the other prophets' writings.
- God's righteousness is witnessed by the Law and the Prophets.
- Paul established his faith and ministry upon what was written in the Law and in the Prophets.

23. In contrast to the more than two hundred times the New Testament deals with prophets, only eleven of them specifically relate to **false prophets**.
24. In comparison to prophecy and prophesying, the prophet as an officer (synonym for ministry) is mentioned many more times. Prophecy and prophesying in the New Testament are mentioned only thirty times together.
25. The traditional evangelical mind confuses prophecy and prophesying with the duties and authority of the office of the prophet, the activities with the functions. The effect has been to isolate, in order to regulate, the predictive tasks of the prophetic from the office and its mantle. This has only been done with one other office, the apostle. The remaining three ministers of Ephesians 4:11 underwent no such severance.

Frequency Statistics Concerning the Prophetic

The following chart shows how much the Lord addresses prophets, a prophet, or the prophetic in scripture. This exemplifies the more than five hundred times the words prophet or prophets are used in scripture; one hundred and seventy of those times are found in the New Testament. It is important to those entering prophetic studies after having spent years in the other Ephesians 4:11 ministers' doctrines.

This non-exhaustive list shows how much the prophetic literally comprise the scripture.

Over the years, many budding prophets and prophetic learners have abandoned their prophetic ministry preparation simply because they cannot reconcile the radical differences between its knowledge and that of the evangelical teachers they have ingested for years.

The list excludes the name and teachings of our Lord Jesus, the Great Prophet who was to come.

Group One

Prophets Named in the Bible	Numbers of Times
Moses	848
Abraham	231
Daniel	83
David	1085
Elijah	99
Elisha	58
Ezekiel	2
Haggai	11
Isaiah	53
Jeremiah	140
Jesus	1540
Jonah	19
Joseph	190
Joshua	200
Nathan	43
Samuel	142
Shemaiah	39

Deborah	9
Miriam	15
Zechariah	33
Total Number Times Prophets Addressed in Scripture	**4840**

Group Two

Prophetic Bible Mentions

Prophet	220
Prophets	242
Man of God	78
Prophetess	8
Prophecy	90
Prophesy	21
Word of the Lord	258
Word of God	50
Vision	103
Thus Saith the Lord	424
Saith the Lord	858
Voice of the Lord	50
Scriptures	53
Total Number Prophecy References	**2455**

Group One		4840
Group Two		2455
	Total	**7295**

This incomplete list represents the importance of the prophetic to God and its validity in every era of humanity. The scriptures themselves are prophetic, being the inspired word of God. The sayings of Christ, while emphatically prophetic, are not counted as they are too numerous.

Value of This Information

The value of this information is to demonstrate for you how little the prophetic mind and ministry of the Lord is known by the modern church and still it is contested. One can hardly quote a scripture, read the Bible, or study the ministry and escape the prophetic. Yet no uniformed place or resources exist for the ministry to grow, become perfected, efficient, or competent at present; even though it is God's most largely addressed ministry in scripture.

Why People Resist the Prophetic

Many times when people object to the prophetic or resist it, they have never truly encountered a prophet or learned enough about the ministry or its mantle to give an educated or insightful opinion on them. This is especially true since the prophetic has been absent from mainstream church ministry for decades. Opposers vehemently reject the ministry and its words as if they have studied or observed it in action for years. Much of the antagonism people have toward the prophetic is third party inspired. They heard a friend's prophetic horror story or their pastors taught them from the pulpit to be afraid of the prophet.

Many of the theological commentaries are written largely by non-prophetic people; the same is true for Bible dictionaries and other Christian study resources. Upon studying them, it is obvious that most of these references present a decidedly evangelical or didactic slant on the ministry, with most of them lacking serious prophetic insight. Based on this truth, often the biggest resistance comes from the fact that people have never really learned what a prophet is and fewer still have had little or no exposure to the mantle in their lives. It is this mindset that today's learners must confront and overthrow in their quest for prophetic wisdom and proficiency.

For the last two decades, the church has been prophesied to by people who have barely, or *never,* read the prophetic scriptures. That means too many prophecies are given in the name of the Lord by those with no sense of their biblical predecessors' foundations. Our prophetic forerunners would never think of doing such a thing. Their commitment to God's word and truth was etched in the very fiber of their makeup. A great example of this is Jeremiah 28:8: *"The prophets that have been before me and before thee of old prophesied both against many countries, and against great kingdoms, of war, and of evil, and of pestilence."* Set aside the tone of the words, and a prophecy against ungodly nations and a powerful principle emerges.

Jeremiah recognized the decadent state of his nation before God, based on his words. Historically the Almighty prophesied doom on national depravity. Since this is what his predecessors did in like situations, Jeremiah had no choice, being a faithful messenger, to follow suit. He was assured of his accuracy because he had studied and well learnt the ministerial mindset of the prophet from the beginning of time. His sense of duty and loyalty saw that he confirmed God's history of not blessing sin so to speak. That is the same burden put upon today's prophets.

The Lord has an entire collection of historical and prophetic writings that show His attitude toward sin and His standing prophetic response to it. From the Lord's perspective, it is divination to bless what the Lord has cursed, a trap many of today's messengers fall into simply by not taking time to know God's words enough to discern what He is saying about a given situation.

Frankly speaking, the matter of prophetic obstinacy facing today's prophets can be summed up under the heading of an evangelical mindset. Theological loyalty breeds a bias that frustrates the prophetic and shipwrecks many a destiny. Most people so cherish their religious heritage that they bristle at any suggestion that it may be flawed or insufficient for them to add prophetic education to it. To learn and execute the prophetic, that mindset must be replaced with God's prophetic mind, something foreign to most of today's Christians. This unrelenting requirement is exactly what you must do if you desire to move into or excel in your prophetic call.

You May Never Have Learned God Prophetically

To be a Christian is to have a unique relationship with Creator God as His offspring because you are born again of His Son Jesus Christ. To belong to someone as a child is to know them in ways youngsters not of the same family know them. That is the case with the Lord God. People know others by how they think, feel, act, and react even before most of these are observed. Children know what their parents like, will approve of, or disapprove of in them and they generally govern themselves accordingly; they obey them. Children, even very young, do not need to be told that mommy or daddy is upset. They sense it because they are party to them and their lives.

A youngster's whole world centers on pleasing mom and dad, courting their favor, and enjoying the best of their parents' attitude toward their children. Here is what the Savior means when He said we must receive the kingdom as a little child. Adult children quibble; older children resent, demand, rebel; but little children trust and believe. They love their parents unconditionally, expecting nothing but love and care in return. That is the way God's kingdom works and it is how His children reap its most bountiful harvest.

The same is true with God's offspring. He gave them His Spirit so that they would have intimate and firsthand knowledge of His ways, thoughts, will, and attitudes.

Scripture says that God gave us His mind in Christ Jesus, Paul writes, "For we have the mind of Christ." Hebrews says God writes His laws in the hearts and minds His children, while 2 Corinthians 6:16 explains His entire goal for the new creation is that He would walk in them, talk in them, be their God and they His people. For someone to become that fused with you, you must be able to hear him or her when he or she speaks to you, know his or her voice, and be inclined to obey what you hear. All three of these fit the classification of prophecy. Essentially, that is what prophecy is. God speaks, humans hear.

However, as you proceed in this training, recognize that you may not know, or have never learned God prophetically and that is why you find it difficult to hear Him speak to you. It is highly possible that you have a strictly evangelical outlook on the Lord that is now being challenged by strong prophetic influences. If this is you, everything the Lord says or does to or through you clashes with your old wine and threatens to strip away your old wine skin. Moving from one stream in the Lord to another is hard and sometimes you feel naked as the old garment is exchanged for the new one.

If that is the case, be aware of the real root of your doubt, resistance, or rejection of these truths. Question their inspiration. If you are totally pastor-trained with no prophetic influences--outside of maybe a few words of knowledge, wisdom, or the gift of prophecy--you will find God's demanding prophetic standards, principles, and actions shocking and not easy to absorb at first. So, give the course time and challenge your reactions before accepting them as genuine. Ask yourself repeatedly who is in fact resisting, and what is there at work in you that is so vehement against the prophetic? Are you responding to one of the many inner voices programmed to filter the knowledge and information streaming into your soul? Here is a list of some of the sources of those voices.

1. The voice of my church
2. The voice of my pastor
3. The voice of my education
4. The voice of my doctrine
5. The voice of my experience
6. The voice of my parents
7. The voice of my culture
8. The voice of my history
9. The voice of my fears
10. The voice of my failures
11. The voice of my belief/unbelief
12. The voice of my successes
13. The voice of my passions
14. The voice of my deepest desire

As you can see, there are many infiltrations to color your view or reaction to prophetic information. These filters act as watchmen over your souls. They are tied to a very elaborate defense system developed by you over the years to see to your comfort, peace, safety, and provision. What motivated you to concoct, sustain, or expand your defense system may take years to surface, but as you go through your development be alert to how sophisticated your network is and how acute its instincts are when it comes to protecting you. When you add the prophetic to the situation, you may find you have very sensitive and therefore volatile reactions to it that flare up without warning or reason. That is why we have devised a program that allows you to meet your defenses head on before they sabotage your ability to succeed in your education, or worse, fulfill your destiny.

CHAPTER TWO

Prophecy, God's Eternal Broadcasts

As an introduction to the study of prophecy, this course begins with the idea of prophecy as God's eternal communications media to lay the foundation for understanding His prophets and prophetics. Nothing better explains the prophetic than the phrase, "God's Eternal Communications Media." What else could better convey the Lord's motive for creating a broadcast medium through which to stream His will, government, intents, and messages to a dark and spiritually deaf humanity?

Another word for *stream* is "to **transmit**," which means, "to send." Synonymous with **communications,** it refers to **broadcasting.** Prophetically applied, the terms illustrate God's way of contacting His world from eternity. In addition, prophecy or prophesying is tantamount to **messaging**; the thoughts, will, ideas and actions of one person produced and formatted to convey (send or carry) to others.

Stream, transmit, communications, and broadcast together give the Lord's prophetic outlook. Collectively through these modes, God streams His eternal messages to communicate

His mind as Creator to this world. Prophecy then is God's medium of communications, which makes prophets His instruments of those communications.

In today's technologically charged environment, prophets as the Creator's equivalent may be seen as His incarnate technology. They serve as eternity's communications terminals carrying and relaying God's messages to His audiences, generation after generation. Now doesn't *that* put the entire institution in a different light? Speaking of light, an appreciation of the ancient world's view of it further explains their awe of the prophetic in ways our era smugly mocks. For not so spiritually obvious reasons, they relied on light for natural and supernatural survival. A journey back into their world helps us to understand why light and its metaphors were so critical to them. Their apparently irrational dependence upon the prophetic seems naive to us today because of its many advancements; modernity appears to have conquered their obstacles. Chief among those things is the power and manipulation of light and light-generated products.

Why Prophecy Equals Light

When one studies the prophetic, one cannot help but be struck by its indivisible link to light and its related metaphors or symbolism. The day, the sun, and moon along with other luminescent metaphors in and out of the Bible repeatedly link prophecy to light. Conversely, its absence is tied to the night and the darkness. Frequently, the inductee to the prophetic is dowsed with light imagery at the start. Upon beginning to receive and convey the word of the Lord, light plays a dominant role in their orientation...but why? The answer is simply because during the time prophecy was making its way into the earth, the source of all light and illumination depended on the supernatural. As it was introducing itself to our natural world, there was no man-made light. This premise is reflected in the angel Gabriel's words in Daniel 12 and the following passages of scripture:

A. **Daniel 12:3** "And they that be wise shall shine as the brightness of the firmament; and they that turn many to righteousness as the stars forever and ever."

B. **Job 11:17** "And thine age shall be clearer than the noonday; thou shalt shine forth, thou shalt be as the morning."

C. **Psalm 80:1** "To the chief Musician upon Shoshannimeduth, A Psalm of Asaph. Give ear, O Shepherd of Israel, thou that leadest Joseph like a flock; thou that dwellest between the cherubims, shine forth. "

D. **Matthew 13:43** "Then shall the righteous shine forth as the sun in the kingdom of their Father. He who hath ears to hear, let him hear."

These passages all connect the heavens, the celestial, and the angelic with light that exceeds the sun or the day. They all use words as metaphors for what it delivers to our world.

Most modern prophets are only casually aware of the rationale that attaches light symbology to the prophetic. What many overlook is the reason it hinges on light similes in the first place. Appreciating *God's prophetic equals light* rationale is important if prophets of today and tomorrow are to remain and become confident of His fulfillment of the scriptures they prophesy until the end of time.

Technology, like everything else in life, has its ebbs and flows. Seasons of enlightenment and prosperity inevitably give way to chaos and calamity where worldwide natural disasters wipe out all human advancement and send humanity back to a dark age. When this happens, the pendulum swings to the other extreme and advancement is replaced with the need for daily survival. All technological emphasis then returns to the spiritual, supernatural, and celestial as the secular bows again to the sacred to learn how to stay alive. Earth's inhabitants, once more confronted with their darkness within, are forced to look outside themselves and the human race for wisdom greater than their own. Their search inevitably points to the Creator's unseen powers for answers to the problems of their physical world and the hidden resources buried in nature.

Prophets should remember that one act of God changes the face of the world in an instant and again places the onus of revelation, light, and illumination back in His control, and forces dependence upon His eternal technology. Revelation 6:12-17 clearly makes this point. When the sixth seal is opened, the heavens, earth, the cosmos, and their ecology are all affected. Earth's topography is obliterated and people are forced to live in caves despite their former status in life.

As if that were not calamitous enough, the heavens are pulled back and the entire planet, no longer rotating as before, see the face of Him that sits on the throne of creation and the Lamb whose wrath is terrifying. For a season, heaven directly imposes itself on earth and humanity as if to prove that neither is anything without it. Light, life, and sustenance all stream down from above to preserve, nourish, and furnish a now devastated planet. As humanity ekes out its daily survival, the world creeps back into civilization. It is especially at these periods in human history that people created to hear from and rightly disseminate the Almighty's wisdom are raised up to carry His truth—a synonym for light—to the world. Their revelations and predictions aid its rediscovery of what chaos and calamity destroyed and concealed beneath nature.

As in the beginning, when this happens, earth's inhabitants are forced to look to the heavens for knowledge, wisdom, and instruction to rebuild and replenish their planet. John's Apocalypse alludes to this recurrence at least three more times before the world ends.

Spiritual Light: The Only Source of Human or Earthly Light

Without God's powerful mega-generator to light our world, light is impossible. That mega-generator is the sun, and since God as with everything else spoke it into existence, creation itself forever enmeshes the prophetic with words. Prophecy brings the unseen into existence; a principle that fortifies the immutable reality that the two, prophecy and illumination, are mutually inclusive of each other. The earth itself has no means of generating its own energy or light. It must get that from the sun. Although the sun has been around a long time, it took the Light of the World's coming to release the hidden wisdom that harnessed God's secret to technologically light and power this world. That is because all energy technology was hid in God in Christ, and when the third Person of the Godhead took up residence in the planet, the light within Him became accessible to our world.

The Holy Spirit's first putting His light in people's hearts enabled them to tap into the light His residence brought into the world. Before that, light was in the world, but men loved darkness rather than the light, says our Savior in John 3:20-21, because darkness alone was in them. The Bible says in Revelation that when the Holy Spirit leaves the planet, it will again be plunged into darkness: the way it was before Pentecost. Do you see how vital God's Spirit is to technology?

Prior to Pentecost, light and illumination were under the domain of God's supernatural creatures, His angels hallowed and fallen. When the angels, the spiritual messengers of the ancient world, began to present themselves to the darkened inhabitants of the earth, its residents' only sources of light were the sun, stars, lightening, and the moon, as the Creator ordained in Genesis chapter 1. Outside of these, there were the natural disasters that emitted a destructive light tied to calamity or other celestial phenomena. The benefits of electricity having yet to be acquired meant early civilizations had no knowledge of how to employ nature's light to remove their darkness.

Over time, though, they discovered ways to light their world with sources other than fire. Eventually they could produce illuminants that enabled them to escape their dependence on the timing of the sun and so extend their workday. That way their day would not have to end at nightfall and they could see to work through the night. Proverbs 31:18 speaks to this: *"She perceiveth that her merchandise is good:* ***her candle goeth not out by night.****"* Aside from torches, what was invented was wax and its slow burning properties. To *illuminate* their darkness, adding another metaphor to the prophetic's light thesaurus, primitive peoples discovered the candle. Later in scripture, the candle became linked to life, the soul, or the spirit.

1. **Job 29:3** "When his candle shined upon my head, and when by his light I walked through darkness."
2. **Psalm 18:28** "For thou wilt light my candle: the Lord my God will enlighten my darkness."
3. **Proverbs 20:27** "The spirit of man is the candle of the Lord, searching all the inward parts of the belly."

Bearing this in mind, is it any wonder that the Bible's metaphors for the prophetic, God and His word, revelation, and all such descriptions center on the effects, imposition, needs, and benefits of light in a very dark world? Reflect on the words of the sweet psalmist David from 2 Samuel 23:4:

"And he shall be as the light of the morning, when the sun riseth, even a morning without clouds; as the tender grass springing out of the earth by clear shining after rain." Also there is Isaiah 30:26: *"Moreover the light of the moon shall be as the light of the sun, and the light of the sun shall be sevenfold, as the light of seven days, in the day that the LORD bindeth up the breach of his people, and healeth the stroke of their wound."* Even today, little can happen without some semblance of light. Jeremiah 25:10 supports this and adds that God's withdrawal of His own light and the people's man- made light is a judgment.

Aside from these passages, another one explains the strong light-prophecy connection. It is from Micah 3:6-7. The scripture establishes light and sight as the key instruments of prophetic transmission and reception. Presented as an act of judgment, the prophet states the Lord turned the prophets' prophecy sources off. What is to be understood from this passage, what was painfully clear to them, was that their source of prophecy was divine illumination. A special luminescence faculty was given to the prophets of the day to enable their prophetics. As a result of their perversion of the mantle, God was turning His prophets' light source off. To us that may seem vaguely unpleasant, if we bother to give it the regard it deserves, but to people whose lives depended upon daylight and moonlight, this was a severe judgment. Any threat of darkness exposed them to all the risks lying in wait for them. Take the following as an example.

A Highway Example

Imagine yourself a highway traveler driving a well-lighted roadway. Think about how comfortable you are because you can travel an ordinarily dark road in the light. What would happen if your road were suddenly plunged into darkness? How long would your comfort level last? How do you feel when you venture into an unlit area of the roadway? Your comfort level drops, your senses react, and you tense up and just want to hurry through that dark stretch of road without mishap. You slow your speed, watch for things leaping out in the dark, and hunt for something to guide your path inwardly rushing to return to the light. That is what it was like for those who lived back in prophecy's formative age. They did not have the safety or speed of your car. They had no paved roads, and on journeys they were always at risk of being ambushed, mauled, robbed, or lost; wandering for days off the main path. Early prophets' audience memories were filled with such experiences, making metaphors depicting relief and protection in the future carry great weight.

To take the example a bit further, go back to your road trip and that very dark road and ask yourself what you have today that the ancients lacked? Besides your motorized vehicle, the answer is streetlights and headlights; they had torches. There it is again, the light reference. The modern world may delude itself into thinking that it is self-sufficient, but truly today's earth inhabitants are no more self-sufficient than were their ancient ancestors. One storm, one astronomical disaster, one major attack from an outside force can so disrupt its power systems that the outages can, for all intents and purposes, throw a community or a country back into the darkness of the Bible days. Should such events occur globally, the whole planet would be just as dependent on sunrise, sunsets, and moonlit nights as the people that were alive during Bible times. The same dark, barren environment would make prophecy mean as much to us today as it did to these early peoples of the world. That is why the prophetic as God's communication's media is timeless.

Those alive today may not find its importance so vital, because of our electrical companies and enormous power supply systems. Still, they all rely on the same thing that the ancients relied on and that is God's light, the sun. Should anything happen to shut off the light source of this world, modern man would be as vulnerable and desperate for natural and symbolic light as were the early civilizations.

They would need to hear from some source outside themselves to answer their darkness with ideas for removing it. Humanity under these circumstances would be just as hungry for spiritual light as they would be for natural light to rediscover its technology. That is why God could reliably link His eternal word to light and all its properties and effects.

CHAPTER THREE

The Absence of Power

Much like earth's ancient eras of existence that were void of light, the prophetic's codes in creation initially depended on supernatural beings to activate their power. The right word, the right sound, and the correct voice could trigger natural events according to what the Lord verbally programmed into creation. There are people whose voices God anointed (consecrated and specially empowered) at creation to activate His creation's hidden treasures and secret powers. Hence, the eternal origin of voice activation or voice commands is in the hands of creatures as well as the Creation.

The one group of people specially prepared for this function in the planet throughout its generations are the prophets. *"And it came to pass at the time of the offering of the evening sacrifice, that Elijah the prophet came near, and said, LORD God of Abraham, Isaac, and of Israel, let it be known this day that thou art God in Israel, and that I am thy servant, and that I have done all these things at thy word"* (1 Kings 18:36). The prophet Elijah understood his to be the voice that commanded the heavens, the earth, and various elements of creation. Other biblical examples include Joshua, who caused the sun to stand still; Moses, whose voice released all sorts of havoc on Egypt; Elisha, whose voice overrode the natural laws of nature; and of course, our Savior, whose voice commanded the elements, angels, and demons.

When the Lord Jesus came to earth to begin His ministry, Simon Peter witnessed the same power in His words and creation's compulsion to obey Him according to Hebrews 1:6: *"And Simon answering said unto him, 'Master, we have toiled all the night, and have taken nothing: nevertheless at thy word I will let down the net.' And when they had this done, they enclosed a great multitude of fishes: and their net broke. And they beckoned unto their partners, which were in the other ship, that they should come and help them. And they came, and filled both the ships, so that they began to sink. When Simon Peter saw it, he fell down at Jesus' knees, saying, 'Depart from me; for I am a sinful man, O Lord.' For he was astonished, and all that were with him, at the draught of the fishes which they had taken"* (Luke 5:5-9).

The Holy Spirit, God's Global Power Source

Today's world would find such feats accomplished by a mere spoken word ludicrous since the outpouring of the Holy Spirit poured out on the earth the powers of light, energy and so forth. Instead, they regard silently pushing buttons and flicking switches to be a better way. But there was a time in history when the only energy humanity had access to was that of manpower. That is how buildings were built, watercourses operated, supplies and provisions were harvested, processed, and distributed. Without natural energy, all motility was achieved by human beings. For instance, people physically fanned their authorities to cool them down, once as prestigious a position as tasting the king's wine and food or speaking aloud on the dignitary's behalf.

All that we take for granted today was once done by the only power the Lord permitted His clay vessels to operate: their own. Ask yourself what it felt like to spend your days waving a fan, stirring water, carrying a brick up or down a rising. How motivated would you be if all you had to look forward to was mechanically providing a comfort or convenience for an elite society member? What if you looked down the annals of time, as many of them no doubt did then, and in your mind you saw no other way of life except being a human machine whose livelihood relied on you to be a human energy supply for another's comfort or safety. That was the BC world of humanity and the early millennia after Pentecost.

Power and the Prophetic

Atomic, electro-mechanic energy was unheard of, as well as any automatic invention. Those heavenly beings that entered and exited the planet at will were the only clue that such a thing existed. These creatures, you will remember, provided the information, special access, or privileges earthly creatures were ordinarily shut out of at the time. How does this relate to prophecy, you ask? It relates in that prophecy was expected to produce a product, to generate something by some supernatural force.

Micah 3:8 implies this: *"But truly I am full of power by the spirit of the LORD, and of judgment, and of might, to declare unto Jacob his transgression, and to Israel his sin."* His words make little sense until you compare them to Mark 16:20: *"And they went forth, and preached everywhere, the Lord working with them, and confirming the word with signs following. Amen."* The two passages link God's word with power and energy; with signs and miracles. Paul being a citizen of that era understood this from his words in 1 Corinthians 4:20: *"For the kingdom of God is not in word, but in power."* Contrary to modern thought, people of that time period valued words. Somehow, they understood that saying was the same as doing and understood it as the rudimentary premise of every authority figure, which is how it became the same for the entire Bible. Words to the ancients were secret, silent energy objects that begot according to themselves.

Words Beget Objects or Events

In BC times, words were seen as more important than anything was. To speak with authority was to make things happen; it answered prayer, averted crises, eliminated danger and distress, and when spoken by the right authority performed the impossible. Jesus' teaching on this wise was not as shocking as we alive today might suppose. His audience was well aware of special individuals that came to the planet uniquely backed by heavenly authorities. For them the rule was simple: the spoken word goes forth and begets a corresponding object or event. The key to that power was understood as coming from the divine being authoring the word. Thus, a prophet had to declare and manifest his or her god and initially acquaint their audiences with that celestial being as the source of their prophetic performance for credibility's sake. That is the essence of the ancient prophet's mantle.

Early prophets' words were not just to be new or revelatory; theirs were also to be words of power and productivity. The visual signage of a prophecy classified a messenger as among the ranks of prophets. They were respected because of the power their words wielded; a power that they were privileged to pull into this world from the invisible one.

A prophet's power was not activated by desire alone, although that may have been the initial catalyst that caused the prophecy to be received and declared. It was understood that a prophet's word was an instrument, implement, or vehicle to make the invisible visible and the unseen seen; that the prophet personified the sending deity.

A genuine prophet was thought to clothe supernatural substances in his or her physical form by simply speaking. Their prophecies became vehicles of performance and those whose words failed to produce themselves in visible form were proven to not be prophets at all. If one gained audience with or were engaged by royalty or another authority, a failed word could cost an impotent prophet his or her life.

Saying Equals Manifesting

The people of the prophetic's formative years highly regarded anyone who could say a thing and then bring it to pass as Job articulates in Job 22:28: "*Thou shalt also decree a thing, and it shall be established unto thee: and the light shall shine upon thy ways.*" The word *decree* as used in the passage means:

1. To cut down
2. To cut off
3. To destroy
4. To divide
5. To decree
6. To snatch

Omer is the Hebrew word rendered *a thing* in the King James Version of the Bible. It refers to:

1. A promise
2. A speech
3. A thing
4. A word

These are all used in respect to something:

- Said
- Answered
- Appointed
- A speech

- A saying
- A word

Relating all these to prophecy answers many questions and frankly says that words were never intended or taken to be idle talk. The ancient world cruelly chided the divine messenger whose word fell to the ground unfulfilled, which is the subtle message of 1 Samuel 3:19. There in his day existed a body of rules and regulations devised to prove a prophet and qualify those claiming to be authentic.

A high-ranking institution in early civilizations, the prophetic carried great weight in society. As a result, prophets were held to strict standards of accountability and judged fiercely if proved wrong. They were expected to be powerful and to possess special license to penetrate any barrier of creation to benefit all those that petitioned them. For these reasons, the prophet was a vital part of the Creator's global power force. See Balaam's authority in Numbers 22:6.

God's Global Power

When it comes to God's global power, earlier worlds were deprived of the visual aids we have today, the main one being the internet. In a time where pervasive global contact and information are commonplace, understanding how God's spirit world operates as a two-tiered single unity should be easier. For instance, it is plain to see in our time how His eternal invisible kingdom appeared everywhere present at once. Instead of words and pictures, angels literally appeared to be everywhere in an instant. The power of that harmonious unity is the Spirit of God.

Although it had yet to show itself in humanity's realms, God's unseen world's energy source was long recognized as the Creator's power to all His creatures. Eternity's immortal beings knew they were empowered by the deliberate and intelligent strength that animated everything the Almighty made. The psalmist says, *"For He spake, and it was done; He commanded, and it stood fast"* (Psalm 33:9). Consider the angel that flooded the Apostle Peter's jail cell with light, and then later, after entering the cell without opening the gates or doors, exited the prison by opening its gates seemingly at will (electronically) to escort Peter out of jail. See Acts 12:7-10.

That intelligence began with God's word; the Bible calls it the *Logos,* which Jesus Christ is identified as being in John chapter 1. God's utterances activate whatever object or appliance in need of motility or utility because He programmed all creation to do so. This is difficult to accept until one tries to come up with one thing that is invented, created, or used apart from words—spoken, written, or thought. Chemicals, instructions, even the genetic structure of human beings all rely on codes that communicate instructions for their actions and effects to come alive. Codes say what a product or object does or is to be when handled or joined correctly with its other complementary components; and they are articulated with words.

A Single Massive Power Source

In our world, such an analogy would target the sun as our main power source whose power, harnessed by our energy companies, feeds our electrical outlets. The cradle of the prophetic did not have this and so a faith in the unseen prevailed to enable them to tap into what they needed. That faith rested in a belief that what was needed existed somewhere and specially chosen people knew how to get it to them. What validated these special people was a covenant with, or skill in coercing, the supernatural agent believed to be in charge of the power or resource sought. Petitioning the right spiritual authority properly gained favor that in turn released the petitioned object. Once more, we see the union of voice, words, and power. Review Exodus 4:8; 15:26; Deuteronomy 13:18 and Psalm 103:20.

A word in a dark era activated energy, and energy relied on the right word from the spiritually authorized voice. Thus, we have the ancient prototype, really the eternal prototype, of "voice activation." Here is where prophecy meets energy (dunamis power) to produce manifestation, the most stringent of all prophetic tests. The ability to manifest what one prophesies was and is the only answer to the question, "Did your god really speak to and through you, and can I trust you to succeed in persuading or releasing your covenant deity to do the same for me consistently? Are you in good standing with the god you are voicing and will my standing with that deity be improved by what you say?" These questions burned in the mind of everyone consulting with a prophet and it is not much different today.

People really want to, in fact cannot help, but rely on the prophet or prophetic types to keep them in touch with the invisible world and its powerful resources. They inwardly crave and almost compulsively turn to one who is not bound to time and space in this world and has met the criteria that enable them to transcend its laws and boundaries.

The Prophet & Voice Activation

Ezra 5:1 and 6:14 give a good biblical example of this in action. The prophets Haggai and Zechariah, each of whom has his own book in the Bible, were assigned by the Lord to help His people rebuild their land. It was hard as the people had heard from those who left their mother country how wonderful it was for years. That is why they leaped at the chance to go back there when the king asked them. What they found, though, was a far cry from what they envisioned. The land had lain desolate for seventy years and it was a mess. No one had worked it and nothing that they were told was there by those that remembered remained. The returnees were disillusioned and overwhelmed. Rebuilding the place was going to take a monumental miracle, and that is just what the Lord gave them in the form of two powerful prophets.

God told His two prophets that had apparently gained a reputation among the people to go and encourage them to begin to build. He wanted Israel rebuilt and the integrity of His word rested upon it. In Ezra 5:1 the prophets begin their task by starting to prophesy life into the workers, faith into the returnees, and favor with the authority. The effectiveness of their prophesying is seen in Ezra 6:14 where it says that the people prospered under the prophesying of Haggai and Zechariah. What a message! The two prophets labored with the workers not merely with hammer and nail but with the word of the Lord. Whatever the workers faced, they prophesied its success until the work was done. They had power with God because they knew their assignment was precipitated by covenant and that Israel's God, a point the writer of the text makes, was backing all their words and their deeds.

In our primitive model, the prophet's relationship with his or her deity in antiquity was founded upon the deity hearkening to the voice of the prophet's word, or better yet, the accurate utterance of a divine word from the prophet's mouth that proved itself by producing corresponding results. That test was passed or failed by how the invisible authority or agent reacted or responded to the prophet's voice. This pattern bears up repeatedly in the ministry exploits of the Bible prophets' chronicles.

From the start of time, God distinguishes His presence by voice. Adam heard the *voice* of the Lord walking in the garden, an enigmatic revelation on its own since one hardly links hearing a voice to walking. Yet that is what the text tells us. God's voice walked and Adam no doubt heard and saw it in motion. Thus, God's voice activated some movement. So embedded are these two realities in God's mind, that Genesis 4:10 says that even blood has a voice. We are told that Abel's voice was still speaking at the time of the writing of the book of Hebrews. That says that blood is empowered by some humanly inaudible voice and intelligence. The writer of the epistle says that Jesus' blood speaks of better things than that of Abel.

Aside from both Abel and Jesus being slain as sacrifices of the Almighty, what the two men also shared was that they are both prophets. Abel is spoken of by Jesus as the first prophet of God to be slain, evidently for the word of God. Jesus comes at the end of the age as the last one to be slain by that generation. See Luke 11:5-52 and Hebrew 12:24. With these two illustrations, the correlation between the voice and action becomes clearer. The prophet speaks and the words manifest themselves in a physical product or event. Hence, sound takes on a form that actuates substance. That is what Ezekiel shows us in prophesying to the dry bones.

To take this principle further, look again at Exodus 4:8: *"And it shall come to pass, if they will not believe thee, neither hearken to the* ***voice of the first sign****, that they will believe the* ***voice of the latter sign****."* In this scripture, the voice is not only connected to a sign but is also presented as a motive of conviction.

The signs themselves, our Exodus reference teaches us, proved to be the literal voice of God translated to action by the events they caused. Invisible servants in the vicinity, no doubt obligated to perform the Lord's words from the prophet's mouth, stand ready to manifest the human form of what is said. In addition, 1 Samuel 15:1 reminds us that the voice sounds words; and for prophets, that is significant since their voices sound God's words in our world. Likewise, the prophet is nothing without God hearkening to his or her voice, what is explicitly stated in 1 Kings 17:22: *"And the LORD heard the voice of Elijah; and the soul of the child came into him again, and he revived."* Also, how the world acts on the voice of God's word is seen in Psalm 103:20. Those invisible creatures, God's angels that we have been talking about, are how God answers the voice of His word. As His unseen celestial agents, they are mobilized by the voice of God's word. See also Hosea 2:21.

Select Voices Compel Creation's Obedience

There are some voices God compels obedience to, and these are those whose sound activates their assigned spheres' forces of creation. Without fail, the prophet's is among these voices. See Isaiah 50:10; Jeremiah 38:20; Ezekiel 1:24.

Together they make the point of this scriptural illustration in Haggai 1:12-14: *"Then Zerubbabel the son of Shealtiel, and Joshua the son of Josedech, the high priest, with all the remnant of the people, obeyed the voice of the LORD their God, and the words of Haggai the prophet, as the LORD their God had sent him, and the people did fear before the LORD. Then spake Haggai the LORD'S messenger in the LORD'S message unto the people, saying, 'I am with you,' saith the LORD. And the LORD stirred up the spirit of Zerubbabel the son of Shealtiel, governor of Judah, and the spirit of Joshua the son of Josedech, the high priest, and the spirit of all the remnant of the people; and they came and did work in the house of the LORD of hosts, their God."* God's prophet's voice is responded to by creation in the same way a voice activated security system or appliance responds to the voice it is programmed to obey. That is why obedience features prominently in effective prophetic behavior and conduct.

Prophets' obedience authorizes their voices to be regarded by God's invisible creation forces. When you see that something was blessed or cursed, it complies with this creation reality. Here is a most primitive creation truth that has gotten lost in today's careless speaking and verbal manipulation. We talk more on this subject later.

A disobedient prophet may get results, but a question arises about the forces that responded and produced those results. *"Then the LORD said unto me, The prophets prophesy lies in my name: I sent them not, neither have I commanded them, neither spake unto them: they prophesy unto you a false vision and divination, and a thing of nought, and the deceit of their heart"* (Jeremiah 14:14). Again, in Jeremiah 2:8: *"The priests said not, where is the LORD? And they that handle the law knew Me not: the pastors also transgressed against Me, and the prophets prophesied by Baal, and walked after things that do not profit"* (Both passages are from NKJV). How does all this happen? Does it really happen, whether we see it or not? The answer to the second question is yes, it really does happen this way. The truth is that it happens very slowly in the flesh since spiritual words take time to acquire and adorn their natural physiques. To answer the first question, it happens by God's angels. The holy angels, the Lord Jesus says, respond to God's holy prophets. These are identified by Him alone because only He can speak to a prophet's overall obedience in and out of the public eye. An errant or rebellious prophet will be abandoned by those God ordained to work with the messenger from creation.

CHAPTER FOUR

The Light From Within

As it happened way back then, the only other sources of light that humans experienced were the lights of sight and vision. Adam's failure caused the source of all the world's energy to retreat in the Person of the Holy Spirit. It did not resume until His return on the Day of Pentecost. Until that time, the world was held in the grip of darkness and under the sway of the wicked one that begot Cain and his offspring. This state of affairs explains two other very essential media of prophecy: eyesight, or vision, and dreams. Once more, the applications are clear. Visions and dreams, other useful terms and elements for prophecy and its revelatory instruments, are historical illuminants that predate modern technology.

For those back in early civilizations, dropping off to sleep in the dark, entering a vision, or dreaming meant something altogether different for the ancient citizen. Seeing into the darkness, receiving information, or otherworldly encounters upon turning in at night was important for numerous reasons. That is why dreaming and seeing visions was prized as more than soulish entertainment. Dreams transmitted visions, as with Nebuchadnezzar in Daniel chapter four. They temporarily breached the ordinary knowledge vacuum of this world and could potentially supply insight, answers, and revelation from the heavens. These spiritual mechanisms were as essential to gathering information then as the telephone, letters, media, and the web are to us today. The spirits could answer questions, reveal secrets, tell historical stories, or supply critically needed intelligence to the traveler, leaders, strategist, or warrior. See the Bible's examples from the following passages of scripture:

1. (Genesis 20:3 KJV) However, God came to Abimelech in a dream by night, and said to him, Behold, thou art but a dead man, for the woman, which thou hast taken; for she is a man's wife.
2. (Genesis 20:6 KJV) And God said unto him in a dream, Yea, I know that thou didst this in the integrity of thy heart; for I also withheld thee from sinning against me: therefore suffered I thee not to touch her.
3. (Genesis 31:11 KJV) And the angel of God spake unto me in a dream, saying, Jacob: And I said, Here am I.
4. (Genesis 31:24 KJV) And God came to Laban the Syrian in a dream by night, and said unto him, Take heed that thou speak not to Jacob either good or bad.
5. (Genesis 37:9 KJV) And he dreamed yet another dream, and told it his brethren, and said, Behold, I have dreamed a dream more; and, behold, the sun and the moon and the eleven stars made obeisance to me.
6. (Genesis 40:5 KJV) And they dreamed a dream both of them, each man his dream in one night, each man according to the interpretation of his dream, the butler and the baker of the king of Egypt, which were bound in the prison.
7. (Genesis 41:7 KJV) And the seven thin ears devoured the seven rank and full ears. And Pharaoh awoke, and, behold, it was a dream.

8. (Genesis 41:15 KJV) And Pharaoh said unto Joseph, I have dreamed a dream, and there is none that can interpret it: and I have heard say of thee, that thou canst understand a dream to interpret it.
9. (Numbers 12:6 KJV) And he said, Hear now my words: If there be a prophet among you, I the LORD will make myself known unto him in a vision, and will speak unto him in a dream.
10. (Judges 7:13 KJV) And when Gideon was come, behold, there was a man that told a dream unto his fellow, and said, Behold, I dreamed a dream, and, lo, a cake of barley bread tumbled into the host of Midian, and came unto a tent, and smote it that it fell, and overturned it, that the tent lay along.
11. (1 Kings 3:5 KJV) In Gibeon the LORD appeared to Solomon in a dream by night: and God said, Ask what I shall give thee.
12. (Job 20:8 KJV) He shall fly away as a dream, and shall not be found: yea, he shall be chased away as a vision of the night.
13. (Job 33:15 KJV) In a dream, in a vision of the night, when deep sleep falleth upon men, in slumberings upon the bed;
14. (Jeremiah 23:28 KJV) The prophet that hath a dream, let him tell a dream; and he that hath my word, let him speak my word faithfully. What is the chaff to the wheat? saith the LORD.
15. (Daniel 4:5 KJV) I saw a dream which made me afraid, and the thoughts upon my bed and the visions of my head troubled me.
16. (Daniel 7:1 KJV) In the first year of Belshazzar king of Babylon Daniel had a dream and visions of his head

upon his bed: then he wrote the dream, and told the sum of the matters.

17. (Mathew 1:20 KJV) But while he thought on these things, behold, the angel of the Lord appeared unto him in a dream, saying, Joseph, thou son of David, fear not to take unto thee Mary thy wife: for that which is conceived in her is of the Holy Ghost.
18. (Matthew 2:12 KJV) And being warned of God in a dream that they should not return to Herod, they departed into their own country another way.
19. (Matthew 2:13 KJV) And when they were departed, behold, the angel of the Lord appeareth to Joseph in a dream, saying, Arise, and take the young child and his mother, and flee into Egypt, and be thou there until I bring thee word: for Herod will seek the young child to destroy him.
20. (Matthew 27:19 KJV) When he was set down on the judgment seat, his wife sent unto him, saying, Have thou nothing to do with that just man: for I have suffered many things this day in a dream because of him.

The Dreamer of Dreams in Society

The dreamer obtained information that guided future behaviors, reinforced or overturned decisions, and answered the perplexing questions of life that otherwise could not be resolved. The prophet Balaam relied on his dreams to get information for the supernatural to carry out his ministry. Refer to Numbers chapter twenty-three. People that dreamed regularly who were able to translate their spiritual communications to the advantage of others were considered prophetic on some level. They could be seers, prophets, psalmists, or dreamers. In all capacities, they served their societies by bridging the gap between the spiritual and natural worlds, meeting the needs of the lower world with the higher one.

In every society, dreamers' communities elevated them whenever they kept them connected with the heavens and its resources. The dreamer's active dream life and skillful dream interpretation brought his or her neighbors vital information from the future to succeed in life. Those encountering seers who could explain visions, as well as solve life's riddles and the enigmas that cropped up in people's dreams, provided tomorrow's answers today. In every era of humanity, they were priceless and prized as essential voices to the community who rescued each generation from the ravages of spiritual darkness. Frankly, today they are received the same way by society, although not always as favorably by the church.

A vision, to explain, came as an answer from someone who was not bound by the day and night cycle of the human experience. Demonstrating they were not bound by earthly constraints, supernatural visitors and vehicles showed up in blazes of light, even in the daytime. For this reason, the writers of scripture often compare their otherworldly visitors and their brilliant apparitions with the light of the sun shining in its strength.

How Sun and Moonlight Worship Began

Ancient people cherished the power and blessings of light (natural and supernatural) to the point of outright worship. See Deuteronomy 17:3 for God's reaction to this penchant. Civilization's early people understood the diminishing shades of the sun's light, how it faded throughout the day. Their era taught them well how to schedule their days so that what needed light was completed before nightfall when no one could work. Hence, is the import of Jesus' metaphoric statement, "the light cometh when no man can work" to describe the only season in which His work can be done. That day, His followers were to learn, was the period of the church age. Review Revelation chapters six and seven to glimpse what He saw happening on earth after the church is raptured. Using their present day, the Lord wanted to reinforce to them that their sustenance and survival relied on accurate assessments of the timing and seasons of their world.

People back then were, of necessity, also intimately familiar with all the elements, protection, and perils of the darkness that refreshed or threatened them daily. The moonlight and its strength became almost as important as the daylight. They were fixated on the waxing and waning moons because it scheduled travel, productivity, and worship and seemed to explain a host of events that occurred only at those times. The moon revealed what was in the darkness, and for the night traveler could be a mysterious savior or a harsh spotlight that crudely expose what lurked in the darkness to take advantage of the night. Criminals and travelers all valued the moon and took care to schedule risky or vital ventures around its appearances. Based on the cultural mindsets that developed at this stage of human civilization, and because of the certainty of the cycles of light and darkness, people became familiar with those spiritual agents that taught them; ritual and religion were born. You will recall that the Bible's rituals were mainly timed with the moon, and so were just as important to their religious calendar as the solar year.

Supernatural Messengers and the Prophetic

Earth's early citizens grew accustomed to the night and its manifestations of those supernatural beings clearly seen back then to be in control of their world and the only means of learning how it worked. Often human in appearance, they were seen as visual expressions of the stars in the heavens and divine representatives of God. The celestial bodies, they surmised, could leave their lofty abodes and visit the earth to deposit a word, inspire a vision or a dream, or simply illuminate an individual at one time or another. They could also show up as instruments of divine judgment or justice. Scripture upholds this, as Jude talks about the angels that left their first estate, supplying a long overdue explanation of Genesis 6:5. In addition, most of the prophets' writings recall supernatural visitations, visitors, and apparitions that provided them with spiritual information and guidance they could otherwise never obtain.

Observed away from earth as lights in the sky, the heavenly bodies taking human form spoke to the people mainly at night, which is why Psalm 19 talks about them uttering their speech at night. Their visitations brought prophecy to the earth to fix it as a standing spiritual tool of eternal truth. Though the stars existed as much in the day as they did the night, it took the withdrawal of the sun to give them appearance and voice and human susceptibility to their sound.

It is under these circumstances and with this mindset that the prophetic made its debut into earthly life and etched its importance in the human psyche. Because of the immutability of the darkness that gripped their world and their vulnerability to it, the prophetic best earned their respect by attaching itself to what they lived everyday. It boasted of answers to the darkness, information from outside their world and times, and revelations about the hereafter, tomorrow, and even the next generation. For sure, there was plenty of room for deception and certainly it abounded, but there must have been more reasons why this powerful eternal resource has persisted down through the ages.

The answer is for all the negativity attributed to it, the prophetic works. It still speaks to and in the darkness. It still performs as effectively as always, illuminating the darkness within people's souls, promising and performing what they could never achieve on their own without it. Prophecy carves the spiritual path that permits heaven-to-earth transactions that bring the eternal into our now and make the impossible possible in a given life. God's angels traverse that path to perform what the Lord commanded His prophets to say in the world about a life or situation whose destiny He has inscribed in creation. Over time, since the dawn of our world, a mega highway system has been constructed in the spirit on prophecies the Lord spoke into the world. This highway is traveled by the angels and other spiritual agents He dispatches to perform His words at their appointed times. Consider Luke 1:20 as a case in point.

Prophecy's proven record of accomplishment lets people know what will be and overturns what apparently cannot or should not be. For these reasons, the prophetic retains its title as the superior bridge between the natural and the supernatural worlds, defending its long standing reputation as the champion tool of the impossible, generation after generation.

Prophecy and Signs and Symbols

We are not yet finished with our journey. Let us get back into our car and return to that highway yet again. This time we want to point out something else that further enlightens our darkness along the way. That something is the sign that directs our paths. Posted with words and symbols, this too looks back to a dark past where people were forced to trust whatever the last traveler left as a marker for those to come. Man-made markers serve the same purpose for the earth, as did the stars in the sky. Travelers were guided by the position of the sun or moon similar to the natural immoveable objects used by the ancients. All these pointed the way to where they wanted to go. Prophecy, too, functions in a similar manner. God marks verbal utterances with spiritual signs, symbols, or natural events to assure their performance in an appointed time, or to confirm their unfolding fulfillment now.

From long ago, symbolism has figured prominently as the cursor of divine truth from the world beyond, and without prophecy that truth is impossible. It presents itself as the purveyor of what people of the day relied on to get through their journeys in life. Symbolism, signs, and natural metaphors such as trees--where anything could hide to attack, or under whose shade shielded the over-heated traveler—made strong symbolism for prophetic allegory. Bodies of water likewise made ready prophetic symbolism because they signified the enduring and what quenched the thirst.

Bodies of water represented crossable boundaries that permitted sea travel or that served as powerful military barriers. The thirsty soldier also appreciated bodies of water because of their glass effect. Stooping down to quench their thirst allowed them to see behind them and notice any enemy warriors lurking in the vicinity. God used this practice to whittle down Gideon's army; see Judges 5:5-7. Seasoned soldiers knew the wisdom of lapping and looking to spot ambushers hiding around them.

To continue, grass as a soft resting place or rocks that could stumble or barricade them made even more ready prophetic signatures. Shrubs and bushes offered food and shielded people from night creatures to be avoided or helped them catch dinner. Either way, shrubbery provided nature's fencing and lent itself well to the language of prophecy.

Integrating nature in their prophecies, which is most unlikely to change or be altered by humanity, allowed early prophets to emphasize spiritual features of their messages that people could relate to help them in life's routine affairs. Man-made imagery was frankly distinguished from what God created as crude, fragile, faulty, and temporal so there was no mistake in the ancient mind about what was enduring and trustworthy and what was transient. When temporality was to be stressed, fabricated emblems were used to indicate what the prophet meant. A fallen tower, shattered vessel or other objects, or destroyed edifice spoke to the Creator's contempt for human accomplishments that bragged they were better than His own were. Christ's prophecy regarding the temple that took forty years and thousands of lives to build, as well as its destruction, are good examples of temporal or transitory prophetic signage. Prophets back then were always careful to depict the sign God wanted to make His point best.

When thinking about the importance of signs and their prophetic link, they were as vital to earlier travelers as those huge markers along the road guiding your car trip today. To greatly understand what the Lord's prophets thought of them, and to appreciate their importance to the Lord's divine communications, reflect on the signs and guideposts that told the pedestrian traveler of old where he or she was in his or her journey.

Those signs that comfort you as you drive your lonely unlit road at night were not there for the ancient traveler forced to rely on the placement of a rock or tree or body of water to trace or retrace their steps. Similar to natural signs, prophecy helps you confirm your direction, desired path, distance, and location in life. Prophecy warns you about dangers and delays that may lie ahead and see that you reach your intended destination peacefully and confidently. Naturally speaking, you rely on signs; you need to know that the mile markers were accurately paced to time your journey and plan your stops. You need to know that the exit identified as the one you want is correct and that there will be a connection to the next highway or a reliable rest stop for you waiting where the sign says it will be. The highway's name or number has to be correct, and those who have gone before you to identify these must be trustworthy messengers. Take these illustrations to the world of prophecy and you can readily see its continued worth to the human life. Messenger integrity, messenger signature, and symbols make or break your road trip and life's journeys. It was no different way back when all ancient travelers had at their disposal were the planets, the stars, and nature.

The Importance of the Faithful Messenger

The prophet's words must be accurate and his or her signs relevant and indelible. The hearer must be strongly impressed to recall the word whenever something triggers it in his or her memory. The prophetic language used to deliver the word must generate for them the best image to depict the sign they received with their prophecy. Messenger integrity was crucial then and it is today. Proverbs 25:13 express the importance of being a faithful messenger. The more faithful the messenger is, the more reliable the message and valuable its instruction will be. Accurate messages are likely to be accompanied by numerous or prominent signs to confirm their prophecies.

Insight into the Ancient Messenger

Again looking back to the days when messengers were strictly word of mouth carriers, this term meant more to the ancients than perhaps it does today. Read the Bible's words on messenger integrity in Proverbs 13:17; 25:13. Messengers of old were more than deliverers of paper and packages; they were literal voices and mouthpieces for their senders. Those that served as more than simple couriers carried the weight and authority of those that sent them. The ancient messenger was directly tied to his or her sender and/or employer to the point of being personified by the message's author. To be a faithful messenger required more than just seeing and saying—hearing and running. It called for a high level of integrity, memory power, right interpretation, and application if one was a high official's delegate. In addition, what was needed was a commitment to truth and accuracy that surpassed many others. Veracity and integrity were the ideal mix for a prominent authority's messaging staff.

In Bible times, the messenger's foremost requirement was the ability to divest themselves of their individual persona to take on totally the identity of the sender of the message they were to deliver. The idea was that what was put in the messenger's mouth by the sender was to temporarily transform the messenger who was to speak it (communicate it) precisely as the sender would do in person if that were possible. Vernacular and dialect aside, the emphasis was on the message and those that delivered it were to do so in order that the hearer brought to mind the sender. The vessel that brought the message was viewed as insignificant to the transmission and every effort was made on the messenger's part to transform himself or herself into the sender for the duration of the dispatch's assignment.

For this reason, many authority figures added to their messages a dimension of enforcement that empowered their messengers with corresponding authority. Doing so was important to certify the messenger's words truly came from the sender named. The messengers were sometimes seen as seals and signs themselves and at other times, they were given items to signify their authenticity. Sometimes tokens were given to the messengers to verify that they represented who they said sent them. These may have included rings or other objects that were the personal possession of the sender. Royals and nobles were known to send their staffs or scepters as tokens of the derived authority their messengers exercised. With prophets, it is the same on the spiritual plane.

In addition, when deities dispatched messengers they too sent with them corresponding signs to be released by their messengers as tokens of the deity's power. The signs were to signify the transference of divine power to the one entrusted with the word of the god's mouth. See Joshua 4:6 as an example. Think about Moses, whose rod exemplified his license to exercise God's authority. Along this line think back to Elisha's rod that was entrusted to his servant to use to resurrect the woman's son. See also Exodus 4:2-4; Numbers 17:2-10; and 2 Kings 4:28-31.

Generally speaking, examples of the messenger of the early world were the stars and their gazers, foot runners, postal carriers, special envoys, or delegates. Those sent on particular errands and assignments at the behest of their senders or sovereigns tended to resort to their signs and tokens for the superior intelligence needed for their jobs. It was believed that all authorities were physical conduits of divine powers and transmitted graces that could be imparted by touch. To be a messenger of such authorities was seen to put the servant immediately in touch with those powers, by proxy.

Summarily speaking, signs, symbols, dreams, visions, and the light serve as prophetic precursors and markers. They operate as the signatory methods and modes of prophetic communication that originally established the institution to forge its essential connection between the seen and unseen worlds. God saw to it that His prophets comprised all these means and methods in living form to make them prophets that is voices and actions that are able to function as His Divine Communications Media.

CHAPTER FIVE

Human vs. Divine Technology

Prophets are God's messengers and since He does everything by His word, all things used by Him must be alive before or at the time of use. Since there is no death in Him, anything He chooses to use starts out alive, even if it is slaughtered to be sacrificed to Him. For God's use, creatures must be presented to Him alive before they are slaughtered to be of service to Him. Hence, alive to die is generally His standard requirement. Qualified humans engaged by the Almighty are those alive to God, vicariously slaughtered by Jesus Christ to become dead to the world. Upon completing their time in the zone of the dead, they are revived, resurrected, and renewed for His employment.

The Lord starts with living beings so it stands to reason that the His counterparts to our telephones, cell phones, satellites, and audio-video devices are embodied in His human vessels; specifically, prophetic ones. That puts the prophetic not behind the world of today but eternities ahead of it.

Before everything we celebrate today as modern technology ever existed, the Creator built into His creation every wonder laid claim to by human inventors. His vast communications network encompasses every aspect of His creaturehood and predates our nouveau marvels by eons. In fact, creation served as the model for all human technology boasted today. That is why to the Lord, human inventions appear primitive and crude no matter how highly they prize and pursue them. The only obvious difference between His creations and ours is that His equipments, lines, cables, and such are start out or remain invisible, spiritual, and pervasive throughout all the works of His hands. All that the Lord made and uses are life, life-filled, and life giving. He is the God of life and the living. His greatest dispensed commodity to a dead, dark world is His life and light. These were priceless to the world of Jesus' day, and they are why His sermons revolved around this theme. If Christ came to earth to minister in the same manner today, He would be less received or believed now than He was then because of technology.

The prophet Ezekiel stressed this one fact when he witnessed eternity's energy, light and motility in the living creations riding their wheel. The prophet makes it abundantly clear in his writings that the dead, dark world of his time was not all there is. He records how the Lord of glory, Israel's God, appears to Him on a living transportation vehicle called cherubim. They appear as self-propelled, all-seeing hybrid creatures with eyes showing up in every part of their being. Heaven's pattern holds true when one looks at the earthly creation. They are in order, do not break rank, and manifest a oneness that puts our sense of unity to shame. That Ezekiel witnessed this sight is phenomenal enough, but that he did so as a Babylonian captive whose consciousness was drenched with the so-called powers of thousands of other gods makes it amazing. The point is made, the God of his forefathers still lives and is the one inducting him into His service by way of these spectacular visions. Israel's God is neither dead nor powerless, but He is the source of all that is and is desired by earth. For someone that has been in captivity to another nation that serves almost anything as god, this experience is life changing. The living creatures are more than images: they are animated. They talk and appear deliberate and focused. These beings are intelligent and Ezekiel knows it.

Creation's Inherent Intelligence

All things created by the Lord have inherent intelligence and their own communications systems. We humans may have to figure it out, but the realms to which the others belong have no problem utilizing their instincts, radars, and inbuilt antennae and so forth to survive and master their environments. It is with these that they gather their food, protect themselves and their possession, and unite to socialize or fight. Their simple behaviors are understood today as intelligence and their acts of reaching out to others like themselves or signaling those who are different may be classified as communicating. Thus the two, *intelligence* and *communication,* go hand in hand with their sending and receiving mediums manifesting as sounds or voices, signs and signals. All of them constitute creature transmissions.

Even now world technologists are struggling to perfect what they call A.I.—Artificial Intelligence. What is your computer but a crude (in comparison to the Creator's technology) replica of how your mind works and processes data? Your computer presently lacks the moral and ethical reasoning and complex thought processing characteristic of the human mind, but it nonetheless does repetitively in an instant what you do without thinking everyday.

The major difference is that what you do well in one area you may not process so well in another. You may out think a computer if you are a math genius and stumble miserably over English, philosophy, and such. The computer has the benefit of the best of every one of its programmers' sum of knowledge on their subjects and disciplines compiled into its memory without the drawbacks (presumably) of human life affairs and daily living responsibilities to distract or overload its processing systems. It does not have to experience being bogged down with the trials and difficulties of life, so its thinking and answering capabilities are unencumbered.

Your computer only has to concentrate on one task at a time, the one you ask of it. You, on the other hand, have to process countless billions of information in an instant on a myriad of subject matter. Unconsciously, you handle enormous life situations, circumstantial details, and tasks at once while still keeping yourself going, in functionally good health, maintaining and building relationships. This you do everyday for perhaps twelve or more hours at a time. Meanwhile, your computer does not have to raise children, build and maintain a marriage, attract and keep good friends, make a living, and grow spiritually, emotionally, and psychologically, but you do. Its systems and programs are simply upgraded when it is time for your computer to service you on a higher level.

All your powerful computer has to do is receive, store, retrieve, and process information. However, its design and architecture comes from you. How wonderfully and fearfully you are made.

Now let's take a look, as a case in point, at your television set. It is no more than a terminal (an end piece of equipment to sound or visualize what has been sent to it). Set in your house it depicts for you distant images received from its transmitter by way of its satellite. Do you see the picture now? *Transmission,* if you will recall, is another word for sending information from a source to a receiver. In this case, that receiver would be your television. The source would be the unit in which its images and content are programmed and dispatched. We will talk more about a satellite later.

Your television shows you what someone else has thought up, processed, and portrayed to send to you on command. You command it by turning it on and turning its channels. When you do, it broadcasts to you what the person who designed or developed what you want to see has to say and show about your subject of interest, or desired entertainment. To be ready when you are to hear or see what they have to send (transmit), the producers of the information you seek must get their messages ready to come to you in a way that you can understand, enjoy, somehow benefit from, and ultimately desire. They must also get them ready in advance, that is beforehand. This is the meaning of the first three letters of the word *prophecy,* which means "to say beforehand." Do you see the connection now? Perhaps that is why Bible scholars think the television or something advanced like it is the false prophet.

Programmers & Programming

What media producers and programmers do to be ready to broadcast or transmit to you in advance is **program** their terminals, instruments, and transmitters to send you what they determined you need to hear or see in the best way you would receive it. So now you see that **programming** is another part of the puzzle, and it is linked to the prophetic. God deposits (the theological term is *imparts)* to prophets what He wants to say through them at an appointed time. For this reason when it comes to the prophetic, times and seasons are very important.

God's prophetic program is His word; His programmers are the Godhead and His angels. His transmitters include the angels, the Holy Spirit, the prophet, nature and the elements, and certain preprogrammed codes triggered in creation at predetermined times. With your television, all your decisions are made for you; you like what you see or you don't. When you don't like what you see, you are told by the programmers and broadcasters simply to change the channel or to turn off your set. What if sound and not sight or the combination of both was your objective, what type of receiver or transmitter would you use to accomplish this goal? Here you would use a telephone.

Like your television, your telephone is a receiver, too. People who want to contact you and communicate with you dial your assigned number and wait for you to answer their ring. They assume your phone will ring until something tells them otherwise. If there is difficulty with the transmission, or what the industry defines as call completion, their pre-programmed alternate systems go into action. Your call is intercepted, rerouted, and/or answered by a phone company representative that explains to you what happened to the call you just placed and why it could not be completed as dialed. Often this explanation comes in the form of a recorded message today; it gives you instructions on how to proceed or recommends that you abandon the call attempt altogether.

For the sake of prophetic relevance, the reason you placed the call in the first place is that thoughts and ideas that came into your mind needed a way to make themselves known to a distant party. Because of distance, you could not say face to face or within earshot what you wanted to communicate to your distant group or party. Therefore, you needed an instrument, a pathway, and a receiver/terminal through which to get what you wanted to say heard far away by the person you wanted to hear it. The telephone allows you to reproduce the sound of your voice on the other end of the transmission.

Naturally, in this scenario questions regarding what the recipient is to do with the call information, or how they were to respond to or act on the call when they receive it, are answered in the content of your message. However, the recipient's decision to accept or receive what you send, or to act on or respond to it, remains their own. That is how it is with prophecy. Whatever decisions hearers make concerning your transmitted messages is theirs. Should there be any corresponding consequences to their mistreatment of the messenger or mishandling of the message attached to the prophecy, they must take responsibility for them as well. If you wanted to address a large group, what type of instrument would you need if they were in the same room with you? The obvious answer is a microphone.

If a message you want to send is to be given to a live audience sitting before you, then the only receivers and terminals you would need to convey your thoughts would be their eyes and ears—more their ears than their eyes. If your voice were not loud enough for them to hear, then you would need another instrument to get your sound to their ears. That would be one of amplification to make your voice louder than normal. Instruments of amplification we all know are called microphones.

All these examples share one constant. Not one of the instruments discussed so far for getting people's thoughts, visions, ideas, and information from themselves to their chosen audiences had any intellectual processing activity required or attached to them. Even if today we are given some opportunity to interact with our communications devices they are still limited in scope and restrict much of what could happen if we were face to face with our audience. With your television, what the sender programmed is what was broadcasted. With your telephone, assuming you dialed the right number, what you say is what the instrument transmits. The same is true with your microphone. It does not correct what you say or how it sounds to the hearers. It simply increases the volume of your voice to the level programmed (turned up to) so your hearers can hear you clearly.

The same principles apply to your pagers. They only collect, disassemble, transmit, reassemble, and reproduce pulses that translate to a number or other invariable information. Your cell phone, instead of using landlines and cables to carry your call and your voice, uses cell sites that pick up your contact from space. The media for it doing so, we understand today, are satellites. Here is where the prophetic shows its excellence over them.

Satellites are giant receivers and transmitters hung in the atmosphere over the earth. They do from space what the old television and radio towers did before them. To bypass the numerous transmission problems associated with terrestrial communications, the satellite allows us to still send and receive our thoughts with little interference from weather, earthly equipment breakdowns, and the like. Satellites facilitate a quick rerouting of all data and signals to the most efficient ground receiver. Wires, cables, paths, and channels are how they send and receive their information and as we have said, terminals are how they reassemble it in an intelligible format that you can understand.

All that was just explained to you to show you how satellites—stars—permit our thoughts to leave the earth, ascend to the heavens, be processed away from our planet, re-assimilate and return to earth at designated destinations. The sender chooses according to the message and the reaction he or she desires where data ends up. The decision to transmit to your television, telephone, cell phone, pagers, or other devices are all based upon the seriousness of the message and the level of response or action it is meant to evoke. While today all these are used to reproduce information transmitted from a distant location to where you are in a format that best gets the message across, before technology they were all carried out by angels and people.

In respect to God and prophecy, as with our important communiqués today, the clarity of the message and its comprehensibleness depend on the coherence of the sender and the quality preparation of the transmitter and receiver.

CHAPTER SIX

How God Prepares His Prophetic Media & Instruments

In prophetic contexts, prophet preparation is the work of the Lord or His angels (also called stars in Revelation 1:20 and 22:16, where throughout the book the main executors of the apocalypse are angels). Prophetic training is paramount to messenger accuracy and integrity. Many activities practiced by untrained prophets may be acceptable, but little of it is excellent. Such prophets yield mediocre results because the more excellent way, in this area, has yet to become widespread.

Mediocrity stems from private devotions contracting prophetic communications without an understanding of what must happen to assure the public transmission of prophecy is intelligible to their hearers. Messengers that want the distinct reputation of becoming excellent prophets must recognize that self-study alone will not achieve it.

God presents Himself to prophets privately. He announces His existence and intentions to them directly and usually during private devotionals times. Rarely does a prophet's first announcement to the ministry come apart from prayer and personal Bible study. Generally, prophecies about the call ordinarily come directly from the Lord who declares that a person is called by him to be a prophet. Public acknowledgements come later in the process.

During their developmental periods, novice prophets only know they are different. It takes outside sources for them to understand that they are different because of being called to the prophetic. God says in Numbers 12:6 that He makes Himself known to His prophets in a vision and subsequently speaks to them in a dream. Both of these speak to private encounters between God and His future messenger. Two words stand out in the passage: **known** and **speak**. Through the vision, God make Himself known (introduces Himself) to His prophets and through dreams, He speaks (communicates) to them. From there a series, really a lifetime, of visitations, excursions, and transmissions ensue that culminate in the novice becoming a full fledge prophet.

Various Prophetic Services Require Diverse Preparation

However, depending upon the duration and extent of the Lord's intended employment of the prophet, training is another matter entirely. Prophets can hear from the Lord, identify His voice, and declare His word without formal training; scripture clearly makes this point. On the other hand, the occupational prophet whose life is devoted to serving as more than an incidental messenger is required to learn much more. Biblical examples of such ministries include Moses, Samuel, Joshua, and Daniel to name just a few. These prophets' ministries involved more than seeing and saying. They were called to lead, shepherd, war, and protect their country and to govern it on behalf of Yahweh, its God. Therefore, independent study and personal self-development are not enough under these circumstances. Hosea 12:10, 13 conveys this to us. *"I have also spoken by the prophets, and I have multiplied visions, and used similitudes, by the ministry of the prophets. And by a prophet the LORD brought Israel out of Egypt, and by a prophet was he preserved."*

Another passage, Psalm 78:70-72, says of David, accepted as a royal prophet to the Lord: *"He chose David also His servant, and took him from the sheepfolds: From following the ewes great with young he brought him to* ***feed*** *Jacob his people, and Israel his inheritance. So he fed them according to the* ***integrity of his heart****; and guided them by the skillfulness of his hands."* The word ***guided*** as used in verse 72 is **"**nachah**"** (naw-khaw); a primitive root meaning, "to guide, transport in order to, bring, govern, lead (forth), into a specified position or place."

David's prophetic work for the Lord went beyond seeing (dreaming or envisioning) and saying (prophesying) His word. Such an assigned range of service calls for broad based training and development that teaches the prophet to handle people, understands their difficulties with theocratic rule, and resolves their conflicts with the Lord's demands for holiness and righteousness. God saw to it that David and His other prophets received His most extensive specialized training, something He did not see fit to do with Saul, Jeroboam, and others He abruptly placed into His service. The higher type of prophet's mantle stays with the people, bears their burdens, and integrates strong priestly, political, didactic, and ecclesiastic functions in routine prophetic duties.

Going After Accurate Prophecies

Scripture tells us that prophecy is likely to come from the Lord directly, or from any one of His angels. A strong factor in delivering accurate prophecy is the messenger's character and integrity. The condition of the prophet at the time of transmission will affect the message to be released by their prophetic voice. A prophet weighed down with sin, hurts, bitterness, the deceitfulness of riches, and the desire for other things can taint or contaminate their messages even though the Lord sent them pure. Their historical state of mind can, by these underlying motivations, turn the truth into a lie or the Lord's righteousness into ungodliness. Training and mentoring help young prophets confront their potential contaminates and exercise their will to override them with God's veracity.

However, it is an established divine principle that whatever is in the heart is what the mouth will speak, says our Savior. That does not apply to involuntary speech only. It also pertains to the word of the Lord deposited in the heart. If the prophesier feels strongly about one thing or another and has not been made aware of these feelings or is denying them, or if the prophet has not been able to relegate opinions to their mantle's revelatory tasks, he or she will have a tough time bringing forth a pure word from God. It does not matter how zealous, sacrificial, or devoted the prophet is to the call.

For example, take the case of your television. If it does not work or poorly translates its communications, no matter how excellent the communicator or the resultant communications, its dysfunction prevents you from getting the message completely or accurately. If a vessel's hearing, interpretive or application skills, character or integrity are weak, it does not matter how exalted or precise the message the Lord sends, by the time you receive it, it will be distorted or garbled when given by the ill-trained or poor character prophet.

In the same way, your telephone when broken, cutoff, or receiving a misdialed number will not complete your call; so will an errant, unlearnt or unskilled prophet impede your ability to get the fullness of a prophetic message from God.

God Counteracts Prophetic Incompetence or Inexperience

Being who He is, God counters one prophet's shortfall with another or even more than a few other prophets. He does this by assigning prophetic tasks to more than one prophet at a time. Taking into account your initial rejection of His word and possible prophet error, weakness, or distraction, the Lord tells several messengers (by several means of communicating) the word He wants you to hear so that you have no reason to say you did not know the will and mind of God on important matters. This is the spirit behind Amos 3:5-8. *"Can a bird fall in a snare upon the earth, where no gin is for him? Shall one take up a snare from the earth, and have taken nothing at all? Shall a trumpet be blown in the city, and the people not be afraid? Shall there be evil in a city, and the LORD hath not done it? Surely the Lord GOD will do nothing, but he revealeth his secret unto his servants the prophets. The lion hath roared, who will not fear? The Lord GOD hath spoken, who can but prophesy?"*

If the Shortfall Was Not the Prophet's

Returning to our earthly analogy, the telephone caller or other sender may have sent the message to the best of their ability but technical difficulties meant you could not or did not receive it. The prophet may have rightly heard God's word for you. The prophecy may have been correctly programmed within to serve as your supernatural receiving device to enable you to hear and use God's wisdom. Nonetheless, that may not be enough to assure you receive the word the Lord sends correctly, promptly, or at all. What is needed is for the prophet to be able to translate accurately to you in a useable format that permits you to act prudently on God's communications. Often this is the missing link between people's prophecies and their ability to understand and apply the Lord's truth. If something obstructs the prophet's reception abilities or the hearer's comprehension, the message perfectly sent from the Father may well fall to the ground unfulfilled. Here is why the Lord puts such emphases on well-trained and thoroughly seasoned prophets. These people do not tend to be hit or miss messengers whose lack of readiness causes much of God's prophetic benefit to His people to be absent. They just fall into it because of the lack of training or the absence of an opportunity to be properly trained. In any case, you the hearer are likely to suffer as a result, despite the ungroomed prophet's pure motives and abject devotion to the Lord.

More on Prophecy Obstruction

Another example of prophecy obstruction is the automatic answering device, which does not have decision-making capabilities. When it receives a message even if it was not meant to receive it, no program tells it to respond with a wrong number message. An answering machine's automated outgoing announcement simply says that the person called is not able to take the call and the caller should leave a message. It does not matter if the call landed with the person you wanted to call. If you reached a wrong number, or if the network wrongly routed your call, it would mean that your correctly sent message encountered delivery problems.

Some interference diverted or intercepted your message and obstructed its destination so the intended audience did not receive the word. The same holds true with your pager, another technological communications device. If you input the wrong address or the end terminal is faulty, you will receive no response to your transmission.

Likewise, prophetic error can cause your prophecy to end up at the wrong place or in the ears of the wrong person. If like your answering machine, the hearer was turned off, overloaded, or faulty, then your very critical or desired message could still be lost to its addressee because technology was not there to relay or receive it correctly.

There are times prophets encounter similarly technical difficulties when delivering their prophecies. People's minds or spirits may be on overload, or saturated with poor spiritual training, or errant in biblical teaching. Any one or all of these conditions may cause them to reroute your words to what they prefer or comfortably understand. At other times, the prophecy may simply be ignored. Lastly, your prophecy may encounter roadblocks set up by previous prophetic experiences.

The Prophet as God's Technological Receiver

In any case, the prophet as God's technological receiver and instrument may correctly receive His prophetic transmission and still find that delivering the message is next to impossible. That is when the Lord inspires this highly intelligent communicator to resort to other innovative means to deliver His word. Some of these may be song, rhyme, poems, dance, drama, or script. Man-made receivers on the everyday level cannot make such reception and delivery judgments and adjustments.

So also with the satellite, if the satellite (star, dream, or messenger angel), is out of working order, to conclude our example, your message may never get to you. In addition, if there is no end terminal (receiving device) for your message to land and re-format itself at your address, you will still not get the word. Are you beginning to get the picture?

CHAPTER SEVEN

Modern Media's Ancient Motives

The most primitive **message transmission** method aside from the verbal messenger is the written letter and its most primitive delivery system is the postal service. Read about how letter delivery got started and was used in transmitting God's word in Bible times from *The Prophets' Dictionary* by this author. It is under message and messenger.

There are yet other types of message transmission media (means, methods, channels, forms, and avenues) to get people's thoughts and ideas from their hearts and minds to our eyes and ears. One of the most popular media today is the movie, if the idea is to entertain one's audience while communicating a message. Did you know that film is a media of message transmission? The story, plot, and script are all enacted versions of what someone wrote down maybe years or decades before to portray to you at some future time. What you see on the screen is someone's impression, beliefs, or suppositions on the subject depicted by the actors. They are normally called characters because they are to impress—imprint—your character, behavior, and conduct with that presented on the screen. Curiously, that is what imprints from your typewriter or computer print is called also—characters—because they impress on the paper what someone thinks in words. Using characters as a means of portraying thoughts and beliefs goes all the way back to those early civilizations we spoke of previously. As far back as religion and history can be traced, people have used drama and acting to portray to worshippers and devotees what the gods of their lands wanted to communicate to them. Ritual reenactments, role-playing, and dramatization are as dated as religion.

Priests, priestesses, ministers, and scribes took what was intangible from the other world and recreated or reenacted it to make it tangible for their tribes in this world. To allow their citizens to hear from their god, conforming their behavior and lifestyles to its will, they spoke, used prophecy, acted out (dramatized), or displayed theatrically what they perceived the deity had revealed to them.

The voice of their communications would be considered the prophet (see Exodus 4:14-17), with whom the prophet and priest (Moses the prophet and Aaron the priest) spoke and dramatized in action as God's revealed will. The entire exodus in scripture is such an example. It was a major cosmic contest between the God of gods and the fallen incarnate gods destroying His earth. Moses' preparation was staged in advance as the Lord trained him for the mission.

The actors or presenters whose images are placed on the film of your favorite movie or portrayed in a live theatre play would be considered prophetic because they take their inspiration and communications from others, presumably higher authorities, and voice them through actions and behaviors. Their character roles say repeatedly and without boundary what the author of their portrayals wrote down in their script. This medium goes all the way back to eternity.

Known to God from Eternity

Scripting for action began with God, who wrote His words for His creation, cast and dispatched them to His invisible creatures—normally His angels—to transmit to the areas of their worlds He assigned them to govern throughout the generations of earth's history. If it is easy to see your entertainment media's practice of taking pre-scripted dramas to portray and transmit to you at their will, it should not be hard for you to accept that the Lord of all creation did it before time began and continues to do so through prophets.

Prophecy is Encoded throughout Creation

Prophecy is encoded in every aspect of creation and responds to humanity mostly by the Lord's supernatural auto-response, auto-play system. Usually the Holy Spirit in the planet activates these, but they can also be triggered by human decisions, behavior, conduct, and beliefs, as well as devils. The Creator's elaborate unseen network has worked so long and works so well that it needs little divine or human initiative to continue to operate. For instance, think about the gospel that preaches salvation to the sinner while declaring God's judgment and correction on the righteous. Both happen repeatedly at the same time. People born into the world hear only the message of the cross while the saved hear the gospel of their sanctification. Those who are being wooed back to the Lord after abandoning Him for the world hear only what is meant for them as the penitent hears in his or heart only the message of the cross that invites them into God's family.

Ministers inducted into Christ's ministry cannot escape the constant pounding of His call that acts as an auto-loop message implanted in their souls, rewinding and playing until they either say yes or emphatically establish that they never intend to obey.

Today, we may receive some of God's divine communication from television and radio, but before then the

Lord got His will through to people via His own technology: prophets, visions, dreams, and angelic visitations.

Human vessels became so persuaded by the mysterious invisible portrayals that they could not help but obey. Amos 3:8 says, "The *Lord God has spoken, who can but prophesy?"* Dreams and visions dramatized to individuals what the Lord wanted them to do. Review for your personal edification the following passages of scripture:

- Genesis 20:3; 6; 31:10,11, 24
- Numbers 11:6
- 1 Kings 3:5
- Job 33:15[1]
- Matthew 1:20; 2:12,13, 19,22; 27:19

Visions as a vehicle of divine revelation are just as frequent in scripture. Twenty times this method is mentioned. See the following:

- Genesis 15:1
- Numbers 12:6[2]
- Job 20:8; 33:15[3]
- Jeremiah 23:16
- Ezekiel, 7:25; 11:24
- Daniel 8:1,2
- Micah 3:6
- Luke 1:22; 24:23
- Acts 9:10,12; 10:3; 11:5; 12:9; 16:9; 18:9

Dreams and visions served today's technological functions before light was ever discovered. Their dramatizations were

---

[1] Establishes the perpetuity of the practice.
[2] Shows both vision and dreams being used by God
[3] See #2.

depicted by eternity's cast to translate into human terms what was being streamed from God's throne. The impetus that triggered these events is the written will and administration of God inscribed in all creation. Refer to the following scriptures to see how they make our point. Eight statements are presented below that should regulate every prophecy spoken by a Christian. They are:

1. Since the world began
2. Before the world was
3. Before the foundation of the world
4. Since the foundation of the world
5. From the foundation of the world
6. Creation of the world
7. Beginning of the world
8. Beginning of the creation

What these phrases share is intricate link to and actual justification of prophecy and the prophets. Matthew 1:22 and 2:5 shows the Lord convincing Joseph, Jesus' surrogate father, that his betrothed was still a virgin although she became pregnant. Returning to the writings of the prophets, the angel says to Joseph that Mary is the one the prophet Isaiah spoke of in 7:19 when foretold a virgin shall bear a son. Review the scriptures below to see how reliant upon them a prophet with integrity must be:

a. Since the world began

- Luke 1:70
- John 9:32
- Acts 3:21
- Romans 16:25

b. Before the world was

- John 17:5

- 1 Corinthians 2:7
- 2 Timothy 1:9
- Titus 1:2

c. **Before the foundation of the world**
- John 17:2
- Ephesians 1:4
- 1 Peter 1:20

d. **Since the foundation of the world**
- Hebrews 9:26

e. **From the foundation of the world**
- Matthew 13:35; 25:34
- Luke 11:50
- Hebrews 4:3
- Revelation 13:8; 17:8

f. **Creation of the World**
- Romans 1:12

g. **Beginning of the world**
- Isaiah 64:4
- Matthew 24:21
- Acts 15:18
- Ephesians 3:9

h. **Beginning of the creation**
- Mark 10:6; 13:19
- 2 Peter 3:4
- Revelation 3:14

At least twenty-four distinct passages of scripture relate the prophet, prophecy, and prophetics to antiquity and before. The Prophet Jeremiah in 28:8 establishes his authority based upon consistency with the prophets of old. Contemporary prophets ought to feel uncomfortable with not knowing their ancient predecessors' writings, sentiments, and revelations of God's truth. Today's prophets should seek to align their words with those that establish the institution from old times, and even eternity.

By now, it is easy to see the prophetic as the Creator God designed and intended as a highly advanced communications system that networks all His living creatures and worlds together to broadcast and stream His words, will, plans, programs, and self-revelation to them at preappointed times. To do this the Lord may blend any creature with a medium, from signs in the heavens (Psalm 19:1) to the signs in the sky (Matthew 16:3 and Luke 12:56); from the everlasting words of His prophets (Luke 24:44) to the evolving events foretold in John's apocalypse.

God Speaks to Everything & Everyone All the Time

The Lord Jesus said, "Let him that hath ears to hear…hear." The Lord, as Job discovered in 33:14-18, speaks to everyone and everything on earth in their perpetual generations. Whatever the situation calls for, like Balaam's donkey, the Lord communicates. Why does He speak? To answer prayers and inquiries; to guide our steps and teach us His ways. God speaks in one way or another to turn us back from the pit and dangerous acts or decisions; to warn us of His judgment, disapproval, or even approval. He speaks to announce to us His will and deeds and to inform us of His intents. The Creator speaks to reveal the past, unfold the future, or explain the present; or even to tell us something pivotal about ourselves. He speaks to tell us what is coming and to prepare us for our part in it as His destiny. These are a few of the reasons the Lord speaks, but know for sure that God speaks to His creation all the time, and those that have ears to hear will hear Him well.

God speaks to rulers before He sets them in power. He speaks to nations to give them an opportunity to enjoy His peace and prosperity. God speaks to demons to warn them and restrain their behavior. He speaks to His family to assure them of His love and protection and to His elements to make them to perform according to His will. He also speaks to the heavens to release or withhold their provisions from the earth (Hosea 2:21). The Lord speaks to sinners to encourage them to abandon their ways for His Son's salvation and to the saint who would transgress the limits of His righteousness, risking His redemption. How does He do all this? As Job says, He does it through visions, dreams, prophecy, and sometimes even life events. Whatever the motive or the means, the Lord is always unfolding His mysteries and destinies to the works of His hands.

The Mystery of Prophecy's Preappointment

Preappointed is a term the Bible alludes to often to let us know that nothing we experience from day to day is a matter of happenstance. For no other group is this a more gripping reality than the prophet. The Lord expects us to understand from its meaning that all life and its epochs are divinely scripted and orchestrated somewhere by multitudes of the Lord's angels and spiritual beings. If you are one who is saved, prophetic, or a prophet, you are embarking upon a call to participant in this massive sovereign network of God's. For extra credit, complete the assignment below.

Glossary of Key Terms

The following are the terms introduced or applied in the book as they relate to prophets, prophetic ministry, the operations and executions of the prophet's mantle.

Agents	One who represents another in business, ministry, and religion.
Ancestors	The family, primarily the fathers, that began a race or a faith.
Ancient	What pertains to the early eras, or before historical times.
Ancient World	The world in which the Bible was recorded and written.
Angels	Celestial beings that oversee and administrate this world.
Antiquity	What pertains to archaic, primordial, primitive times.
Astronomical	What pertains to the stars and the heavenlies.
Authority	The lawful right to enforce obedience that alters behavior.
Auto-Response	Self-triggering answers and reactions.
Balaam	The rebel prophet that served God for money until Moses instituted Israel's prophetic ministers.
Bible	The 66 books of writings that record God's history with earth and man, and His eternal promises and provisions for those He redeems.
Blood	The red color of the life fluid of all

	mammals that religions, especially pagan, drank and offered to solicit favor from divine beings. Jesus' blood shed for humanity closed this practice to the spiritual world forever. Until then, the blood of animals was accepted by God to atone for human sin.
Broadcasting	A synonym for streaming and transmitting; the prophet's word released to the world.
Candle	The first source of domestic light; symbolizes the human spirit.
Celestial	Another word of for angels and other invisible heavenly beings.
Charismata	The word for the operation of spiritual gifts bequeathed by Jesus to His church by the Holy Spirit.
Cherubim	The name of a type of heavenly being said to guard and praise God's glory.
Church	The body of Christ increased by the new creation, also called the ecclesia.
Church Leaders	The ministers, especially the five-fold delegated authority over the church of Jesus Christ; includes bishops, deacons, presidents, and ministers.
Civilizations	The society of scripture that helped shape and activate prophecy in the Bible's formative years.
Codes	A body of signs, symbols, tokens, or a set of rules and laws that permit access to God's invisible realms and allow prophecy to motivate the supernatural and thereby become effective.

Commandments	The set of orders, directions, ordinances, and legislation that comprise God's governmental will for humanity and earth.
Commentaries	Annotations, analyses, comments, and notes that clarify and interpret its subject matter to improve learners' understanding.
Communication	The system of codes, transmission, and language used to deliver a message.
Cosmic	The Greek term for world.
Creation	The term used in scripture to identify the sum of God's handiwork in the planet, including humanity.
Daniel	One of the three apocalyptic prophets; he has a book named after him. The other two such prophets are Zechariah and Ezekiel.
David	Israel's second king from whose lineage the Lord Jesus descended in His arrival to earth.
Day	Prophetically used to indicate or symbolize newness, freshness; the season of light or the life of a thing, event or person.
Decree	A rule, judgment, declaration, pronouncement, verdict, or announcement.
Deity	A word used for a divine being that is celestial and sometimes terrestrial.
Demons	The word used for the fallen angels that occupy and evilly manipulate this world.
Divination	The acts and words of invisible beings taking advantage of their spiritual status of existing outside of time. Divination is

	the word for false or carnal messages they deliver in advance, giving information on human life and its impending events; that is, when the words are not contrived to deceive the gullible.
Divine	Another word for heavenly and spiritual beings as distinct from humans that are mortal, or doomed to die.
Drama	A word to describe prophecy's role in decreeing, portraying, and staging events to develop and emerge from their prophecies.
Dream	Dramatic portrayals that visualize and act out a spectacle during a person's sleep.
Dream Interpretation	The acts and processes of explaining and applying a dream to a human life situation or to address a particular earthly circumstance despite its origin, spiritual or carnal.
Dunamis Power	The super human ability, energy, force, and power received by the church and its individual members from the Holy Spirit.
Elements	The essential components and basic parts of an object, subject, or process.
Elijah	One of Israel's major prophets renowned for bringing great reform, confronting and destroying Jezebel's false prophetic staff, who escaped death by being whisked to heaven in a supernatural chariot. This was proven by his appearance with Moses at Jesus' transfiguration.
Elisha	Elijah's pupil and successor.
Encounters	An ancient term used to identify a

	human's meeting with a divine being.
Energy	The power of life and productivity.
Enigmas	The riddles, mysteries, and puzzles of life that prophets, such as Daniel, are presented in the Bible as being able to solve.
Enigmatic	What reflects or emerges from enigmas.
Eternal	What is outside of humanity, this world, and its limitations belonging to the realms and spheres of God.
Eternal Messages	What God says or does that He scheduled in this world to be revealed by His prophets and other vessels of prophecy in time. His messages can include beside prophets, nature in its absence or inadequacy, and the heavens.
Eternal Origin	What has its beginning in God' world as timeless that affects the physical world.
Evangelical	What pertains to the preaching and redemptive ministry of the evangelist, the third minister of the Ephesians 4:11 staff.
Evangelism	The acts and words an evangelist preaches to inspire repentance and motivate salvation.
Ezekiel	One of the three apocalyptic prophets of the Old Testament; Zechariah and Daniel are the other two. Ezekiel is a major prophet with a priestly mantle.
Five-Fold Ministers	The name given to the five New Testament church ministers that the Apostle Paul understood from Jesus was to supervise and administrate His church. They are called in Ephesians 4:11 as apostle,

	prophet, evangelist, pastor, and teacher.
Foundations	The ground or premises of a particular line of thoughts, beliefs, teachings, processes, or activities; the fundamentals of a study or discipline.
Gabriel	One of the two angels specifically mentioned in the Old Testament. Gabriel is the angel of prophecy, and the one that decrees and initiates earth's national leadership changes according to his visit with Daniel to give him his apocalyptic prophecy.
Gazers	Shortened form of stargazers; a biblical term for astrologers or crystal ball readers.
Generation	The era or age of a particular group of people, which live and affect the world in a given era.
Global	Another word for orb, round, circular; also a synonym for the world.
Gods	A word the Bible uses for divine (immortal, though not necessarily eternal) beings with authority over peoples, nations, human spheres of activity, or territories.
Government	The rule, administration, and control of a body, organization, country, or group; includes laws, policy, regulations, statutes, and the order of people that handle them.
Great Prophet	Another name for Jesus, who Moses foretold would come as the last Old Testament prophet that reminisce his powerful, one-of-a-kind prophetics to complete God's plan to save the world.

Hebrew	Another name for Israel and the Jews.
Highway	A paved road traveled that serves a city or other civilized community.
Holy Angels	The title God and Jesus gives to the angels that chose not to defect to Satan's revolt against the Most High.
Holy Prophets	The title God and Jesus gives to the prophets that faithfully serve the Godhead according to His pattern of prophetic ministry.
Holy Spirit	The third person of the Godhead that integrates the Father and the Son's presence and ministry in the earth.
Imagery	Icons and visuals of one thing to illustrate another.
Images	Pictorial signs that say one thing in place of another.
Instrument	An object used to achieve a purpose, function, or activity.
Intelligence	Knowledge, understanding, insight, and foresight that processes and presents information that benefits others or that enable competent action.
Judgment	A decision rendered between two possibilities upon which penalties or rewards are based or crimes are exonerated.
Kingdom	The rule, possessions, and authority of a king or other monarch.
Law & the Prophets	The phrase the New Testament uses to identify the scope of God's government, adjudication, and revelation.

Manifest	To show, uncover, emerge, exhibit, and demonstrate something that would or could otherwise be overlooked.
Mantle	A symbolic word for the ancient covering worn by prophets and other leaders in scripture. Today used metaphorically to indicate the order and level of a minister in biblical terms.
Media	A means by which something is accomplished or a communication is transmitted.
Messenger	One that carries news, reports, and communications from one person to another.
Metaphors	Words, phrases, or discourses that image one thing to describe another.
Moon	The light of the night sky that serves as the sun's satellite believed to possess and emit special powers and godlike authority; worshipped by ancient peoples and pagans today.
Moonlight	The light of the night that shows at designated times of the month. Ritualistically, petitioned for its supposed divine presence and magical ability to benefit humans on earth. The moon is typically credited with goddess power due to its monthly cycle of waxing and waning since the word *moon* means month.
Moses	Israel's most renowned prophet that led Israel out of Egypt, set up the nation's government under God, and who appeared to Jesus on the Mount of

	Transfiguration with Elijah.
Mysteries	Initially, a religious word to describe hidden knowledge and secret rites practiced by a religious order.
Natural Signs	Images of or in nature credited with supernatural power, ability, or authority.
Nature	The word given for the physical world that encompasses plants, vegetation, animals, the ecology, and the heavens.
Network	A word used to describe a set of connected people, objects, or wires. When pertaining to people it is synonymous with an association. Prophetic networks are called *companies* in the Bible.
New Testament	The twenty-seven books of the Bible that follow the Old Testament's thirty-nine books. They are the four gospels, the Acts of the Apostles, and the epistles. The New Testament distinctive is that it is written by, or narrates the activities of, Christ's apostles in much the same way that the Old presents the words of God's prophets.
Novice	A newcomer to a field or group.
Pastors	The fourth of the Ephesians 4:11 offices designated to oversee a single or group of church bodies called congregations or assemblies.
Pentecost	Meaning fiftieth, the word used to identify Old Testament festival of first fruits and the day the New Creation church was born.
Peter	One of Christ's twelve apostles chosen to found His church; initially the head of its

	Apostolic Council in Jerusalem.
Phenomena	A series of miraculous, unusual occurrences that signify, symbolize, or betoken a noteworthy supernatural event. The presence, working, or authority of a divine being's involvement in a prominent earthly affair.
Planet	The earth, world, a globe, or similar object in the heavens that is part of this or other solar systems.
Predictive	Saying beforehand what will happen; a typical definition of prophecy.
Primitive	Ancient, archaic, prehistoric.
Principles	A main belief or ruling ideology.
Prophecy	God's word, will, thoughts, and intents voiced in this world.
Prophesier	One who prophesies irrespective of being called to the prophet's office.
Prophesying	The acts and content of uttering prophecy.
Prophet	The second member of the Ephesians 4:11 staff responsible for predictive, revelatory, declarative messages and actions associated with divine governing duties.
Prophet Functions	The work, tasks, duties, and prophetic operations that pertain to the office's purpose.
Prophet's Ministry	The term used to identify the range of prophetic work and service to God and His church.
Prophet's Voice	The sound and words that come from the prophet's spirit anointed with the power and authority to move the Lord's invisible

	beings, objects, and agencies to perform in the physical according to His will.
Prophetic Behavior	The distinct deed, manners, and conduct that indicate one is a prophet, or reflect what the Bible prophets did that served God's government and sustained His people.
Prophetic Benefit	The advantage of blessings and good that characterize a prophet's work and word.
Prophetic Call	The Lord's means of inducting the prophet into His service by the Holy Spirit.
Prophetic Duties	A phrase that classifies a prophet's responsibilities in God's service and in the world.
Prophetic Education	The distinct training and development those called to the prophet's office undergo to equip them for competent service.
Prophetic Experiences	The sum of heavenly encounters, episodes, and transmissions that empower and endow prophets to achieve God's purposes in their generations.
Prophetic Link	Before time revelatory connections between a prophet's word and subsequent events that come about as a result.
Prophetic Message	Prophecy or prophetic activity exercised by one occupying the prophet's office on God's behalf.
Prophetic Mind	The mind that hears, discerns, predicts, and reveals what the Lord thinks, feels, and communicates to the earth.
Prophetic Performance	The acts, practices, and executions of the official prophet or one assigned to act or

	speak by the Holy Spirit.
Prophetic Signatures	Spiritual symbols, images, and tokens used to affirm prophecy or confirm the fulfillment of a prophet's word.
Prophetic Tasks	An assignment, delegation, or duty given by God to be carried out by a prophet or one acting temporarily by the Holy Spirit in an official's stead, particularly a prophet's.
Prophetic Transmission	The program of studies or prophecies delivered by a prophet as part of the mantle's communication and broadcast duties.
Prophetic Types	People that exhibit classic prophetic (seer, predictor, revelator, watcher) character, interests, and aptitude as demonstrated by their conversation, conduct, and behavior.
Prototype	An origination of anything that forms the pattern by which all others in its class are molded; includes samples, examples, and types of the original.
Psalmist	A person inclined to spiritual genre put to song or used to foretell the future; applies to David and other poetic, prophetic, and musical revelators.
Realms	An earthly territory or jurisdiction distinguished from a sphere, which signifies an invisible one.
Receiver	An instrument that picks up or takes in information from an outside, usually distant source.
Regulations	A set or system of laws and policies that legalize or standardize policy, procedures,

	products, formulas, or behavior by making them conform to the set rules of a particular order.
Religion	A body of teachings, beliefs, and rites a group of people has bound themselves to adhere to and perform, based upon their founder's encounters and persuasion with a particular deity or the supernatural.
Revelation	What uncovers existing truth that enlightens learners, seekers, and worshippers.
Revelatory Instruments	Vessels, media, sources, and people used to acquire revelation, the uncovering of hidden or submerged truths.
Riddles	Puzzles, conundrum, and challenges meant to tease the brain, solve mysteries, answer difficult questions, or otherwise pierce the veil of the unknown to obtain secret information.
Ritual	A set formula of activities and objects practiced and offered to appease a deity, knowingly or not.
Roadway	A strip of land used by travelers' vehicles or those traveling by foot.
Royalty	The term used to describe leaders of monarchical lands. Can also refer to males or females as kings and queens or princes and princesses, their offspring.
Rules	A legal, judicial or policy-setting system used to govern and regulate a people, organization, or territory.
Sacrifices	The slaughter of an innocent victim performed to appease a deity or to

	advance one to a specially defined maturity.
Samuel	A transitional prophet that represents God's shift from priest, teacher, and Levitical rule to the prophetic just prior to the commencement of Israel's monarchy. Samuel is the last of Israel's prophets under its judge system.
Satellites	Besides being a synonym for angel, a transmission object installed in the sky to send and receive information from and to earth.
Scripture	The term for God's holy word inscribed on paper; what is called the Bible.
Security System	Noise-making or light-emitting objects that warn, alert, or notify of danger or other serious condition. Prophets serve as God's spiritual security system in the world, especially over His people.
Signs	Words, symbols, and images that give direction, inform and instruct, or indicate one thing for another.
Similes	Descriptions of like comparisons that use one idea or thought to explain another that is similar to it.
Simon Peter	One of Jesus' original twelve apostles; the first head of the early church's Jerusalem council.
Skill	A special ability achieved by practicing a given talent or act enough to become competent and/or proficient at it.
Solar	The sun and what relates to it.
Spiritual	What is outside this world, above its laws

	and limits, and thus supernatural.
Standards	The system of criteria that measure achievement and success according to a prescribed system of values and performance levels.
Sunrise	The end of darkness and beginning of the night season. Prophetically refers to breakthrough and new beginnings or eras viewed as instrumental to a certain way of life.
Sunsets	The end of daytime and the onset of darkness. Prophetically, applied to the end of a period, era, time or season viewed as instrumental to a certain way of life.
Supernatural	The otherworldly that is not necessarily heavenly or godly.
Symbolic Light	Languages, images, or expressions meant to enlighten or reminisce light.
Symbolism	The effects of select words, events, and markings intended to call to mind something literal that they represent.
Symbology	The study or practice of using, interpreting, or relying on symbolism.
Symbols	The actual words, events, and markings intended to call to mind or represent something literal that they are meant to represent.
Teachers	Those that communicate knowledge and perfect skill and ability by way of instruction, lectures, examples, and exercises.
Technical	Procedural methods used to normalize a repetitive operation, productivity, or

	action to render it routine and so reliable.
Technology	The science or practice of devising and perfecting techniques associated with inventions.
Telephone	A means of voice communication that allow the voices and thoughts of others to be heard at distant locations instantly.
Television	A means of visual communication that transmits sounds and images through a box wired to receive and send them to viewers.
The Law	The Ten Commandments given by Moses, and their subsequent applications, that are meant to preserve, empower, and enhance the human life experience in God's community. Luke 24:44 says they testify of the Messiah and form the basis for His ecclesiastical canon.
The Psalms	The one hundred and fifty hymns, praise, poems, and prophecies written by David and others to commemorate their experiences with God, His promises to them and the world, and testimonies of the coming Messiah.
The Prophets	A phrase used by Jesus on several occasions to indicate the line of prophets that spoke to God's people, established and defended His law, and represent Him as the living righteous word of God. These are counted from the foundation of the world until its end.
The Sun	The brightest light supplier in this solar system.

Theological	What is related to a deity and its word.
Theology	That which pertains to a deity as its thoughts, teachings, self-revelation, and desires for its offspring.
Tokens	Objects that symbolize or serve as omens, or other types of representations of a coming event.
Transmission	The acts and processes of sending information from a source to a receiver. Prophetically, prophecy spoken by the Lord to His prophets and declared by them qualifies as His divine transmission.
Transmitters	Objects and instruments that transmit (send information) from one place to another distant one.
Unseen Powers	Invisible agents and beings Created by the Almighty to govern, cause, and control the events and activities in this world.
Unskilled Prophet	One that is untrained, whose prophetic words are untried, and whose prophetic performance is moderately or intermittently successful.
Vision	A view or observation of sights and scenes otherwise undetectable by the physical eye, or that are observed while asleep.
Voice	The sound of words, thoughts, or actions that when uttered, allow the ears to hear.
Voice Activation	Pre-programmed instruments and operations that move and perform at the sound of a voice.
Voice Commands	The encoding of equipment, objects, and instruments that goes into action at the sound of a particular voice. Prophetically,

	this applies to the world's oldest and most advanced technology: that of the prophets that actuate creation when they utter the Creator's words as He ordained and commands.
Watchmen	Another word for prophet; it specifically, relates to prophets. The word watchmen speak to God's staff of surveillants that exercise the protection and defense duties of the mantle.
Wisdom	The word the Bible uses for the sum of God's communications to the world upon which all its activities, knowledge, learning, and systems or patterns are based.
Worship	The means by which a deity is praised, revered, thanked, and otherwise celebrated.

Index

Printed in the United States
55223LVS00002B/61-69